HILLERMAN
Country

♦♦♦

HILLERMAN

Country

✦✦✦

A JOURNEY THROUGH THE SOUTHWEST WITH TONY HILLERMAN

PHOTOGRAPHS BY BARNEY HILLERMAN

HarperPerennial

A Division of HarperCollins*Publishers*

To Margaret Mary,
who taught us to keep the crayon inside the lines.

First published in 1991
by HarperCollins*Publishers*
10 East 53rd Street, New York, NY 10022

Designed and produced by Weldon Owen Inc., 814 Montgomery Street,
San Francisco, CA 94133 Tel (415) 291-0100, Fax (415) 291-8841

Text © 1991 Tony Hillerman
Photographs © 1991 Barney Hillerman

Weldon Owen Inc.
Managing Editor: Jane Fraser
Assistant Editor: Ruth Jacobson
Design: John Bull, The Book Design Company
Map: Stan Lamond, Lamond Art & Design
Production Manager: Mick Bagnato

HarperCollins*Publishers*
Publisher: William M. Shinker
Executive Editor: Laurence Peel Ashmead
Editor: Eamon Dolan
Production Editor: Anne McCoy

First HarperPerennial Edition

The Library of Congress has catalogued the hardcover edition as follows:

Hillerman, Tony.
  Hillerman Country / text by Tony Hillerman ; photography by Barney
Hillerman. — 1st ed.
    p. cm.
  ISBN 0-06-016400-X (cloth)
  1. Southwest, New—Description and travel—1981– 2. Southwest,
New—Description and travel—1981– —Views. 3. Southwest, New—
History, Local. 4. Hillerman, Tony—Journeys—Southwest, New.
I. Hillerman, Barney. II. Title.
F787.H53 1991
979.—dc20   90-56349

Paperback ISBN: 0-06-092446-2
Production by Mandarin Offset, Hong Kong
Printed in Hong Kong

A Weldon Owen ◆ Production

*Right: Anasazi storage bins built into a cliff near the San Juan River,
southern Utah.*
*Pages 2–3: Sandstone shapes in the Acoma Valley, with Seama Mesa in the
background.*
*Page 4: Ship Rock. On its 7,178-foot-high pinnacle, the Navajo Hero Twins
killed the Winged Monster.*
*Page 5: Mare and colt with the throats of old volcanos beyond, near the
Arizona-Utah border.*
*Pages 6–7: A basalt dike, relic of an extinct volcano, produces a waterfall in
southwest Colorado's San Juan Mountains.*
Following pages: The first snow of autumn shades the San Juan foothills with white.
Page 12: Aspens warn that summer's over in the Colorado San Juan Mountains.
*Page 13: A red-winged blackbird, usually seen in flocks of hundreds, enjoys a
solitary moment at Bosque del Apache.*
Pages 14–15: Sandstone buttes on the Navajo Reservation.

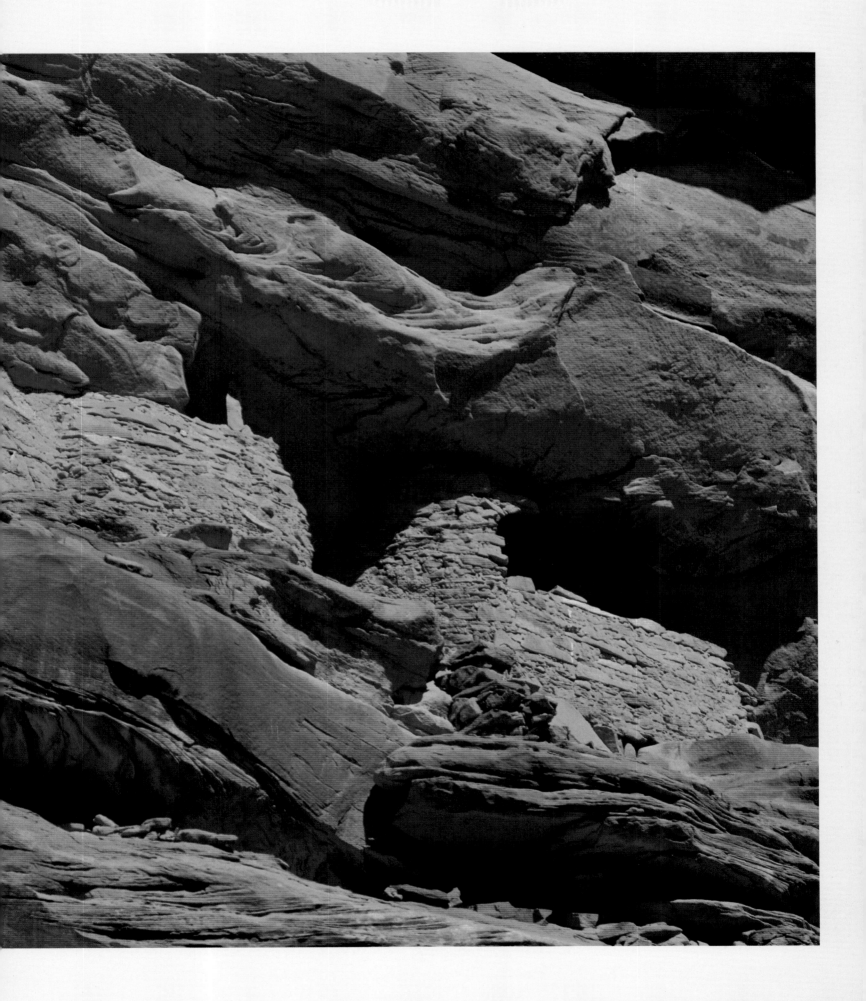

CONTENTS

◆◆◆

INTRODUCTION

◆◆◆

I t's hard to draw a precise boundary around the territory that makes me feel particularly at home. The Automobile Club of Southern California included the heart of it in its "Indian Country" map, which covers parts of New Mexico, Arizona, Colorado, and Utah. And Indian country it is—the home territory of Navajos, Utes, Hopis, Zunis, Lagunas, Acomas, Papagos, Havasupais, and Apaches (be they White Mountain, Mimbrenos, Jicarillas, or Mescaleros), or the string of Pueblo people who occupy their fifteenth-century villages up and down the Rio Grande from Taos to Isleta.

But to take in all the country I favor, you have to extend the map—southward down the Tularosa Basin and the Rio Grande valley toward Mexico and northward into the high meadows of the southern Rockies. Much of it is included in what eastern mapmakers once called The Great American Desert. Much of it is part of the Colorado Plateau, or inside what we locals call Four Corners Country. All of it is high and dry, lacking the rainfall that makes valleys green, cattle fat, and people rich. And over it all arches the vast high country sky—dark blue in winter, hazy with dust in the spring, and in late summer noisy with dramatic thunderstorms.

Above: Horno oven with assorted prairie flowers.
Left: The view of southwestern Colorado from Mesa
Verde, enjoyed by the Anasazis before they
abandoned their cliff homes there.

Seventeenth-century adobe church at Laguna, with vapor trail.

It is distinctly American West, as opposed to American East. In my mind, America West begins near the 100th meridian, the boundary being determined mostly by the climate. If you have a window seat on an afternoon flight westward from such eastern cities as Boston, Des Moines, or Dallas, you can see it below you. As you cross the Texas Panhandle you notice under the wing of the jet that something has been changing. You are flying out of the vast river of wet air that flows up from the Gulf of Mexico, bringing the rains which make America's flat midlands the breadbasket of the planet. You are flying into the Pacific wester-lies—winds that have been dried by a thousand miles of mountains and deserts. The cloud cover, the dim haze of moisture, is thinning below you. Press your cheek against the glass and look forward. You see earth rising out of the humid air like the headland of a continent emerging from the sea.

You can see it from the highway as well, even though the transition seems less abrupt. An hour or so west of Amarillo on Interstate 40, the smooth green wealth of the winter wheat fields gradually gives way to broken country. Towns are smaller, poorer, farther apart. To the south lies Llano Estacado, the "Staked Plains" that once were the domain of the Kiowas and Comanches. To the north lie the "High Plains." (There Barney's and my mother, as a girl, homesteaded a claim to 160 acres of prairie. In this woodless landscape, where desiccated cow and buffalo chips were the only source of fuel, she and her brother would sometimes take a wagon ride to a creek where three cottonwoods grew—a nostalgic trip into a childhood enriched by shade trees.) As you drive westward over these plains you drive into drier country. You see less cultivation now, and the green gives way to the grays and silvers of the desert. There is more cactus, buffalo grass, Indian rice grass, and grama, fewer cattle, more erosion. The land rises into the "caprock country," where undulate sand dunes form on the leeward side of hills.

You have left the easy, fertile, prosperous country behind you. Ahead lies a landscape not designed for human occupancy. The cliffs of its buttes are too steep for climbing. It is too dry, too broken, too empty, too stony for anyone's comfort. The air is so clear now, so free of the humidity of lushness and prosperity, that mountains are outlined on the horizon, sharp and blue, while they are still hours away. And all above you, there's the incredible western sky.

I've lived under that sky for two-thirds of a longish life and it still has the power to stop me cold with its cloudscapes. I stand and stare and marvel at the majestic beauty reflected and refracted light can produce in what is nothing more substantial than mist.

Ponderosa, juniper and sage on the Jicarilla Reservation.

He was watching the dust storm moving down the valley with its outrider of whirlwinds. One of them had crossed a gypsum sink, and its winds had sucked up that heavier mineral. The cone changed from the yellow-gray of the dusty earth to almost pure white. It was the sort of thing Emma would have noticed, and found beauty in, and related in some way or other to the mythology of The People. Emma would have said something about the Blue Flint Boys playing their games. They were the *yei* personalities credited with stirring up whirlwinds. He would describe it to her tonight. He would if she was awake and aware—and not in that vague world she now so often retreated into.

From Skinwalkers

♦♦♦

Hopi basket.

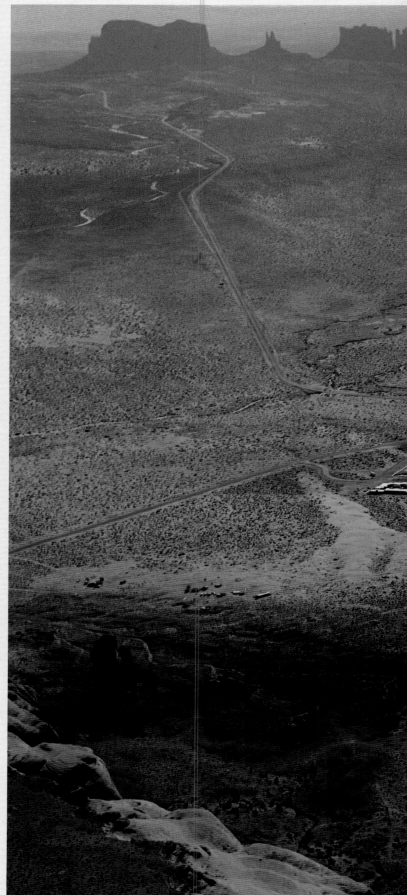

Navajo consolidated school near the entrance to Monument Valley.

Now that I think of it, mist sometimes comes close to drawing a precise boundary to the part of the country I'm talking about. Fog is rare in this environment. But it sometimes forms in patches on mountain slopes when hot sunlight follows thunderstorms. There it catches in the tops of evergreen forests, suggesting smoke from smoldering fires.

Fog forms more dramatically when high-pressure systems bulge out of Canada into the central plains. The Rocky Mountains bar the heavy cold air they carry from spreading westward, forcing it to rise, climbing the eastern slopes. At the top of this mountain barrier, the cold collides with warmer air moving eastward across the desert. Thus, looking eastward from Albuquerque, you see along the crest of the Sandias and extending southward down the ridge of the Manzano Mountains as far as eyesight permits, a wall of high-altitude fog. In the summer it usually hangs on the mountaintops, obscuring them and rising a thousand feet above, as if God had decorated the tops of the ranges with an infinity of cotton. In the winter when the temperature gap between the cold east and the warm west is greater, the heavy air sinks slowly down the mountainside, and the cold mist pours down Sandia Mountain's granite cliffs like a silent, slow-motion waterfall. Usually the mist vanishes in the dry western air before it sinks into Albuquerque's Northeast Heights. When it doesn't, Heights folk awake to find it has settled around them and beyond, sliding downhill into the river bottom. You look down from the high residential areas over a Rio Grande valley filled with fog. Until it burns away, the light of the rising sun makes it a dazzling white line snaking southward toward Mexico.

With some exceptions, that white line forms the eastern boundary of my kind of country. The Land of Little Rain. The Place of Room Enough and Time. Empty Country.

◆◆◆

*A*utumn along the road down from Wolf Creek Pass.

he sun had gone down behind the San Francisco Peaks and turned the bottom of the clouds that hung over it a luminous salmon-pink. The mountain, too, was contested territory. For the Hopis, it was Mount Sinai itself—the home of the kachina spirits from August until February, when they left this world and returned underground where the spirits live. For Chee's people it was also sacred.

From The Dark Wind

♦♦♦

*H*opi Kachina doll

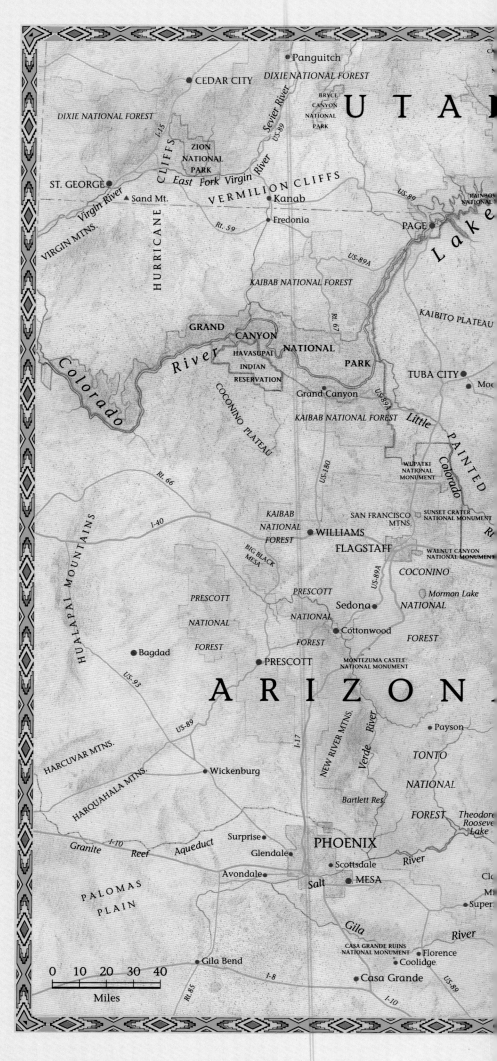

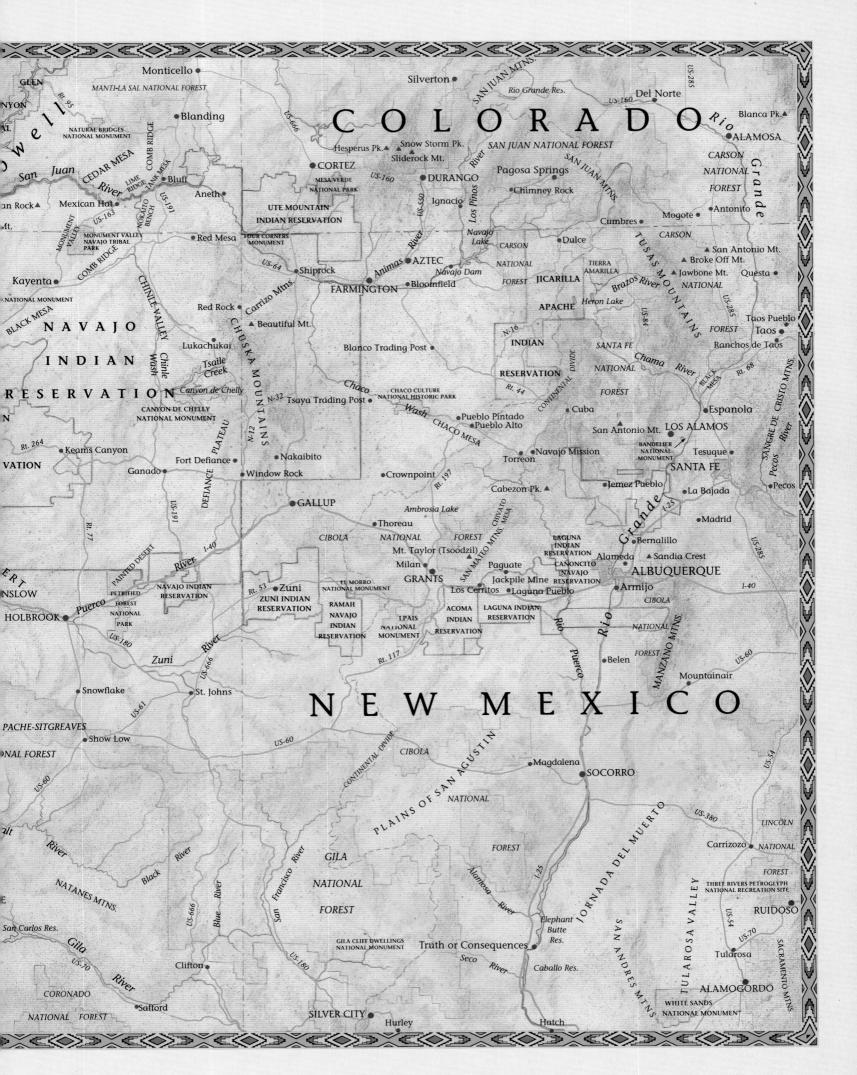

GLEN
YON
AL
Monticello
MANTI-LA SAL NATIONAL FOREST
NATURAL BRIDGES
NATIONAL MONUMENT
Blanding
Silverton
San Juan Mtns.
Rio Grande Res.
US-160
Del Norte
US-285

COLORADO
Rio Grande
Blanca Pk.
ALAMOSA

CARSON
NATIONAL
FOREST

CEDAR MESA
COMB RIDGE
Bluff
Hesperus Pk.
Snow Storm Pk.
Sliderock Mt.
CORTEZ
MESA VERDE
NATIONAL PARK
US-160
DURANGO
Pagosa Springs
SAN JUAN NATIONAL FOREST
Chimney Rock
San Juan
River
Mexican Hat
LIME RIDGE
NOKAITO TANK MESA
Aneth
US-191
US-163
US-550
Ignacio
Los Pinos
SAN JUAN MTNS.
Mogote
Antonito
Cumbres
CARSON

MONUMENT VALLEY
NAVAJO TRIBAL
PARK
Red Mesa
FOUR CORNERS
MONUMENT
Navajo
Lake
CARSON
NATIONAL
San Antonio Mt.
Broke Off Mt.
Jawbone Mt.
Questa
TUSAS MOUNTAINS

Kayenta
COMB RIDGE
US-64
Shiprock
Animas
River
AZTEC
Dulce
FOREST
JICARILLA
Brazos River
US-84
NATIONAL

NATIONAL MONUMENT
Red Rock
Carrizo Mtns.
FARMINGTON
Bloomfield
Navajo Dam
TIERRA
AMARILLA
US-285
Taos Pueblo
Taos
Ranchos de Taos

BLACK MESA
CHINLE VALLEY
Beautiful Mt.
APACHE
Heron Lake
Heron Lake
SANTA FE
Chama River
FOREST

NAVAJO
Chinle
Wash
Lukachukai
Tsaile
Creek
Blanco Trading Post
N-16
INDIAN
NATIONAL
BLACK
MESA
Rt. 68
SANGRE DE CRISTO MTNS.

INDIAN
Canyon de Chelly
CHUSKA MOUNTAINS
Chaco
RESERVATION
Rt. 44
FOREST
Espanola

RESERVATION
CANYON DE CHELLY
NATIONAL MONUMENT
N
N-32
Tsaya Trading Post
Wash
CHACO MESA
CHACO CULTURE
NATIONAL HISTORIC PARK
Pueblo Pintado
Pueblo Alto
CONTINENTAL DIVIDE
Cuba
San Antonio Mt.
LOS ALAMOS
Tesuque
Pecos River
Pecos

DEFIANCE PLATEAU
Rt. 264
Keams Canyon
Fort Defiance
Nakaibito
Rt. 212
Navajo Mission
Torreon
BANDELIER
NATIONAL
MONUMENT
SANTA FE

VATION
Ganado
Window Rock
Crownpoint
Rt. 197
Cabezon Pk.
Jemez Pueblo
La Bajada

GALLUP
US-191
Ambrosia Lake
CHIVATO
MESA
LAGUNA
INDIAN
RESERVATION
Bernalillo
Madrid
I-25

Thoreau
CIBOLA
NATIONAL
FOREST
Mt. Taylor (Tsoodzil)
SAN MATEO MTNS.
Paguate
Alameda
Sandia Crest
US-285
Rt. 77
I-40
Milan
Jackpile Mine
CAÑONCITO
NAVAJO
RESERVATION
ALBUQUERQUE

Rt. 53
Zuni
EL MORRO
NATIONAL MONUMENT
GRANTS
Los Cerritos
Laguna Pueblo
Armijo
I-40

PAINTED DESERT
River
NAVAJO INDIAN
RESERVATION
ZUNI INDIAN
RESERVATION
RAMAH
NAVAJO
INDIAN
RESERVATION
LPAIS
NATIONAL
MONUMENT
ACOMA
INDIAN
RESERVATION
LAGUNA INDIAN
RESERVATION
CIBOLA
MANZANO MTNS.

ERT
NSLOW
PETRIFIED
FOREST
NATIONAL
PARK
Puerco
NATIONAL
FOREST
Rio
Rio

HOLBROOK
US-180
River
Rt. 117
Puerco
Belen
US-60

Zuni
River
Puerco
Mountainair

Snowflake
St. Johns
US-666
US-61

NEW MEXICO

PACHE-SITGREAVES
Show Low
US-60
CONTINENTAL DIVIDE
CIBOLA
Magdalena
US-54

NAL FOREST
US-60

GILA
NATIONAL
FOREST
PLAINS OF SAN AGUSTIN
NATIONAL
SOCORRO
LINCOLN
NATIONAL

ult
River
River
Black
River
San Francisco River
FOREST
Carrizozo
FOREST

NATANES MTNS.
Blue River
US-666
GILA
NATIONAL
FOREST
Alamosa
River
I-25
JORNADA DEL MUERTO
SAN ANDRES MTNS
TULAROSA VALLEY
THREE RIVERS PETROGLYPH
NATIONAL RECREATION SITE
SACRAMENTO MTNS.
US-54
RUIDOSO

San Carlos Res.
Gila
River
US-70
GILA CLIFF DWELLINGS
NATIONAL MONUMENT
Truth or Consequences
Elephant
Butte
Res.
Seco
River
Caballo Res.
US-70
Tularosa
US-380

CORONADO
Clifton
US-180
Hatch
WHITE SANDS
NATIONAL MONUMENT
ALAMOGORDO

NATIONAL FOREST
Safford
SILVER CITY
Hurley

THE DINEH AND THE TURQUOISE MOUNTAIN

◆◆◆

T he white man's name for it is Mount Taylor—a worn-down Pleistocene-era volcano about sixty miles west of Albuquerque. The same weakness in the earth's crust that produced it has been the scene of scores of other eruptions. Thus Mount Taylor is surrounded by a cluster of smaller monoliths, about a hundred basalt necks of minor volcanos, by twenty-five square miles of hardened lava flow, and by lava-capped buttes.

The Navajo name is Tsoodzil, the Turquoise Mountain, the southern pillar of the four sacred mountains that mark the boundaries of Dine'Bike'yah, Navajo Country. In Navajo metaphysics it has existed since God created this layered universe. It was there in the darkness of the First World, and in the sequence of worlds through which the beings who would become Navajos continued their evolution. In the physical form I now see on the horizon sixty-five miles west of my home, it was built by First Man, one of the mythical Holy People, the *yei* (spirits) who serve as teachers and intermediaries between God and man.

For twenty-five years my daily homecoming from the University of New Mexico took me off the eastbound I-40 freeway at the Louisiana Avenue exit. As I'd reach the overpass from

*A*bove: *Lizard hunting northeast of Tuba City, Arizona.*
Left: *The view from above timberline on Mount Taylor*
across the Laguna Reservation.

the exit lane, Turquoise Mountain would appear atop the guardrail. The shape is changeless, of course, but the appearance varied with the hour and the season. When still autumn air traps Albuquerque's smog in the Rio Grande valley, the mountain seems to float above this haze as if the magic knife First Man used to secure it to the ground had slipped. With winter, the peak turns white. Tsoodzil never seems to look quite the same, but it always turns my mind away from the city to thoughts of fir-spruce forests, and a spirit called Blue Flint Girl who lives there, as Navajo ritual poetry tells us, "in a house made of morning mist, a house made of dawn."

Empty as my favored landscape is of people, it is well populated with spirits, and it was these, literally as well as metaphorically, who called the Navajos home from captivity. Some seven thousand of the tribe, held at Bosque Redondo in eastern New Mexico's Pecos River valley for four miserable years, persuaded General William Tecumseh Sherman to let them go home. Like the Hopis who came before them, they preferred their "ashheap of desert" surrounded by their four sacred mountains to any material wealth the whites might offer.

It was May 1868. Sherman had given the captive tribesmen a choice. They could stay on a reservation at the place where they had been interned since the winter of 1863–64, or they could move to land in the fertile and game-rich Arkansas River valley of what is now Oklahoma. If these sites were unacceptable, they could return to their high, dry corner of the Colorado Plateau. But the fertile part of that would be denied them. Their best farm and grazing lands had been seized by the whites. What was left to them had been devastated by Colonel Kit Carson, his U.S. Army troops, a newly Americanized Mexican militia, and their Ute allies. Carson's strategy had been a campaign of scorched earth and winter starvation. All Navajo shelters and supplies were burned, orchards chopped down, and livestock that could not be driven away as plunder were slaughtered. Nothing useful was left behind. General Sherman warned the Navajos that he doubted they could survive in the desolation that had been left them.

Fallen timber shaped by high-altitude winds, on the slope of Mount Taylor's Mosca Peak.

It was a rare opportunity for a people to choose between material welfare and the values of the spirit. The proceedings of the Peace Commission record the decision. Clan headman Barboncito spoke for the Navajos: "I hope to God you will not ask us to go to any country but our own," he said. "When the Navajos were first created, four mountains and four

Tsoodzil (Mount Taylor), the sacred Turquoise Mountain of the Navajos, as seen from the rim of Acoma Pueblo's lofty mesa perch.

Following pages: Acoma Pueblo atop its mesa.

Cactus beside the lava flow, Tularosa Basin, New Mexico.

rivers were pointed out to us. That was to be our Dinetah, and it was given to us by Changing Woman [a principal Holy Person in the Navajo order of spirits]. It was told to us by our forefathers that we were never to move east of the Rio Grande or beyond the San Juan."

Outside of the four sacred mountains, Barboncito said, "whatever we do causes death." Lightning killed them, he said. The Pecos River drowned them. Even their friend the rattlesnake struck them with no warning in this foreign place. The rituals they had been taught by the Holy People for curing their sick would not work outside the four mountains. Away from the beauty of their Dinetah homeland there was nothing but sorrow.

"The mourning of our women makes the tears roll down into my mustache," Barboncito said. "I can only think of Dinetah. I am just like a woman, sorrowful like a woman in trouble. I want to go and see my own country. If we are taken back to our own country we will call you our mother and our father. If you should only tie a goat there, we would all live off of it, all of the same opinion. I am speaking for all of the People, for their animals from the horse to the dog, also for the unborn."

He was indeed speaking for all the Navajos. The transcript of the Peace Commission shows that a vote taken the next morning was unanimous. The treaty was signed the same day. General Sherman wrote President Andrew Johnson that while he thought the tribe might starve in the rocky expanse of canyon and desert left to them, it was land so worthless and desolate that they should be safe at last from the greed of the white men. He called this desert reservation "as far from our future possible wants as it is possible to determine."

The Navajos began their long walk home the day after the treaty was signed. Barboncito, Narbona, Ganado Mucho, and the others of the advance party reached the top of the pass between the Sandias and Manzanos on July 4, 1868. Navajo legend tells us that when these old warriors crossed the pass in the Manzano Mountains just east of the Rio Grande and saw the ragged blue shape of Tsoodzil silhouetted by the sunset on the horizon, "tears of joy ran down their cheeks until their hands holding the reins of their horses were wet with them."

I don't remember the date I first drove past Tsoodzil on old U.S. Highway 66, but it was late summer 1945, probably in early August. Northwest of the mountain that same

Rabbitbrush in bloom below a Navajo shaman's ridgetop cairn.

The old Hubble Trading Post at Ganado, Arizona.

afternoon, my path first crossed that of the Navajos. World War II was winding down. I was an infantryman just home from Europe, with a patch over my left eye, a stiff leg, and a sixty-day convalescent furlough. At a U.S.O. dance in Oklahoma City I had met a girl whose father had two trucks loaded with oil well drilling equipment parked in his yard, but no drivers. He offered me a job hauling a load to some nameless place on the Navajo reservation in western New Mexico. I took it. I had never before been west of El Paso.

I now know that those first Navajos I encountered were participants in a curing ceremony. They were "the stick carrier's camp" en route to deliver the symbolic "scalp" to the patient's hogan as part of an "Enemy Way" ritual. All I knew then was what I saw—a group of mounted men and women emerging from a thicket of piñon and juniper and crossing the dirt road ahead of my truck. There was a trail there, I'm sure, but it wasn't visible from where I stopped, and the riders seemed to emerge as if by magic from that great cliff of pink-and-salmon sandstone that forms the southwest wall of Mariano Mesa. Some of them were in ceremonial attire, painted and dressed as warriors returning from the mythic raid on which the ceremony is based. The lead rider carried a feathered pole to which a long-billed cap was tied. I learned later that the patients being cured were two marines who had come home to their people from the battle of Okinawa. I presume the cap was a trophy taken from a Japanese soldier.

If my memory is dependable under forty-five years of rust, I left the equipment at a drilling site somewhere north of where the Tsaya trading post now stands. Even now this is an empty corner, and in such lonely places any stranger is interesting. As we unloaded, a rancher came by to find out what was going on. I told him what I had seen. He explained it. This was a seven-day ceremony ending with a "squaw dance" tonight and a "scalp shooting" a little after dawn tomorrow.

Could I attend?

Well, maybe. Such ceremonials were family affairs, he said. Friends, relatives, and fellow clansmen of the two cousins would be expected to be there to help the cure with their good thoughts. Strangers usually didn't come. But Navajos are hospitable people. If I was sober and behaved myself with dignity, I would probably be welcome.

That squaw dance and that scalp shooting linger in my memory. My imagination has transmuted them, as imagination does with good memories. Gradually accumulated knowledge of Navajo metaphysics has illuminated them, giving religious meaning to what

Four Corners Navajos wearing traditional attire for tourists.

*Following pages: Hopi farmer at work
at Moenkopi, Arizona.*

The afternoon clouds had formed over Black Mesa, far to the south, producing lightning and air turbulence. As far as Chee could estimate from thirty miles away, no rain was falling. He studied the cloud, enjoying the range of blues and grays, its shapes and its movement.

From *Skinwalkers*

◆◆◆

*A*nasazi painted quiver.

*T*wilight falls on the town of Chinle, with Black Mesa in the background.

38

Turquoise Mountain where the Navajo Hero Twins slew the Walking Monster, seen across the malpais of lava flow formed by the monster's dried blood.

I saw. I still remember the bonfires lining that packed-earth dance ground, the dust raised by shuffling feet, the flickering yellow firelight, the perfume of burning piñon and juniper, the sparks blown by the night breeze, the four drummers, the smell of roasted mutton, and the two marines—exhausted, but happy to be cured of war and home again—surrounded by their friendly people.

*M*alpais southwest of Grants, New Mexico—the lava colored by lichen growths.

Since that incident in 1945 the country west of the Rio Grande has provided me with a head full of such scenes and special places. Many have become the nucleus from which a story has taken shape. That curing ceremony became a crucial part of the plot in *The Blessing Way.* Tsoodzil, the wilderness of lava beds below it, and the mixture of people, cultures, and religions flourishing around it inspired *People of Darkness.* If I were forced to name my single favorite place on this planet, I think it would be that turquoise mountain.

From where I live in Albuquerque I can look toward the sunset and see Mount Taylor serene on the horizon—blue enough with distance to merit its turquoise name. As the crow flies, it is about sixty-five miles away, and I enjoy the thought that I could leave my car at the last house on the west side of Albuquerque, stroll into the sagebrush and snake weeds toward it, and reach it with hardly a fence to cross and almost nothing to remind me that I don't have the planet to myself. Nothing, that is, but the white lines the transcontinental jets draw across the sky six miles up and, at night, the glow of Albuquerque's city lights behind me reflecting off the cliffs of Sandia Mountain.

At the end of such a walk, I would have reached Tsoodzil.

Long before the Navajos declared it their Turquoise Mountain and the southern guidepost to their homeland, the Pueblo Indians living along the Rio Grande and west of it had given it names and mythology to conform to their own religion. To some of them it is Dark Mountain, where one of their War Twins lives to warn people away from dangers of the western desert; to others it is the access route linking the world of men with that of the Kachina spirits. Then the Spanish came and called it Cebolleta (Little Onion) Mountain. Finally, the United States of America named it after one of its least memorable presidents, Zachary Taylor.

*F*ollowing pages: Cliffs near Ghost Ranch, New Mexico, where Georgia O'Keefe loved to paint.

The theory of its origins are as varied as its name. In the cosmology of the Rio Grande Kachina religions, it was part of the earth as originally created. Our geologists think it is much younger—the product of volcanic activity in the Pleistocene era not much more than a million years ago. The Navajos, typically, deal with it in the poetic metaphor of the Dineh Bahane, their Book of Genesis.

For them, as with the Pueblo tribes, it had existed from creation, originating in that first Black World where living consciousness began. It reappeared in Second, Third, and Fourth Worlds, along with all those primal concepts which would evolve into bluebirds, badgers, corn beetles, coyotes, snakes, and humans. Finally, it was built in its "outer form," which I see as a blue hump on the western horizon, by First Man as a cornerstone of this Fifth, or Earth Surface, World.

First Man, the original story tells us, spread a blue blanket on the earth and built the mountain using material brought up from the Fourth World, which had just been destroyed by a cosmic flood. He decorated Tsoodzil with turquoise and assigned another *yei*, Blue Flint Girl, to live on its peak, guarded by Big Snake and serenaded by First Bluebird. But what we see of Mount Taylor is merely its "outer form." Its "inner form" (and the "inner forms" of the three other sacred mountains that mark the boundaries of the Navajo cosmos) has existed since the Creating God started the ticking of time.

I like to visit Turquoise Mountain in late summer. Mosca Peak, the highest point, rises to 11,300 feet. That's modest by standards of the southern Rockies, but it stands alone on the south end of the Chivato Mesa highlands. Thus it is both a landmark and a mother of thunderstorms. In August the prevailing westerlies push moisture up from the Gulf of California. Clouds build over the mountain most afternoons into towering, anvil-topped formations. They break free and drift eastward, trailing rain across the Laguna and Canoncito Navajo reservations. Then, in the empty sky left behind, another cloud forms in the mountain updrafts and the process is repeated.

The U.S. Forest Service built a lookout tower atop Mosca Peak and a road winding through the spruce and fir forests to service it. Around the turn of the century, a fire swept across the slope below the peak and left behind a jackstraw tumble of logs. Generations of new growth have been encroaching on this old burn, and now the wilderness of fallen timber

*B*luebirds in the southern Rockies.

Stratospheric winds spread a fan of ice crystals from an "anviltop."
Usually rain produced by such desert clouds evaporates before it reaches the thirsty earth.

The Turquoise Mountain seen across Laguna Pueblo grazing country.

Mesa, lava malpais and a bite or two of grazing on the Laguna Reservation. Following pages: A blue water playa in the malpais east of Grants, New Mexico.

is green with an undergrowth of mountain mahogany, skunk cabbage, lupine, columbine, aspen, and all those grasses, herbs, and bushes that thrive in mountain ashes. On the fringes of the burn, the forest is reasserting itself in thickets of young spruce and fir.

On afternoons when Tsoodzil is birthing one of its thunderstorms, the gray mist collects over this tangled meadow and catches in the tops of the firs. Fog obscures the spruce. The Forest Service road disappears. The air, always cool at this two-mile altitude, takes on a chill. All those almost-forgotten aromas that the dry desert air is too thin to carry emerge and reach the nostrils. You smell pine resin, the perfume of flowers, decaying leaves, damp grass, and the ozone produced by lightning. Even on sunny days it is a quiet place. Fog produces such total silence that you become conscious of your own breathing, even of your own pulse. Whatever external sound reaches you is oddly muffled. The occasional thunder bumps and thumps around you. The call of the owl back in the blue spruce seems unnaturally low-pitched. Electricity building toward the next thunderclap raises hairs on the back of your arms, making you happy to be down here among the fallen timber and not exposed on the ridge of Mosca Peak above. There the "Thunderbird" would kill you with a stroke of lightning.

Navajos studying to become *shaman* come to Tsoodzil and to the other three boundary mountains to collect soil, minerals, and herbs needed for their *dah nidiilye'e'h*—the deerskin prayer bundle (or "four mountains" bundle) of items required in the curing rituals they will conduct. If you find a painted stick decorated with feathers planted amid a cluster of plants or propped among the boulders, it was probably left as an offering to replace a plant or a fragment of stone that was taken.

In Navajo theology, Tsoodzil is a sort of combination of Western society's Mount Sinai, Mount Parnassus, and the Dome of the Rock. It is the base point for a gigantic (if invisible) Rainbow Man *yei* that circles almost a thousand miles from here to Blanca Peak in the Colorado Sangre de Cristo Mountains, then westward to Hesperus Peak, and then south to the San Francisco Peaks above Flagstaff, Arizona. Rainbow Man is the protective spirit that, supported by the four sacred mountains, encloses Dine'Bike'yah, the Navajo Country.

These same mountains are also the points where the hands and feet of Mother Earth touch those of Father Sky.

Tsoodzil gains even more importance in Navajo cosmology as the starting place for the epic campaign of Monster Slayer and Born for Water. In the Navajo account of human genesis, monsters infested this Earth Surface World. They had been born in the underground Fourth World as a result of violation of sexual taboos and had followed the Earth Surface People into the Fifth World, slaughtering them until, when the two Heroes arrived, only a few survived.

*Cholla cactus thrive where an abandoned
ranch house founders behind the Jemez Mountains.*

*M*iners' houses at Madrid, New Mexico, fifty years after the mines closed.

*R*esidence at Acoma, a town that competes
with Hopi Orabi for the title of the nation's
oldest continually occupied town.

53

Weather erodes sandstone into ice cream shapes on the Acoma Reservation.

The Hero Twins were born of a union between the great *yei* called Asdzaa Nadleeh (Changing Woman) and the Sun. They visited their father in the sky and stole from him magic weapons. On Tsoodzil the twins stalked and outwitted Yeiithosh Lai (One Walking Monster). Monster Slayer shot it with an arrow of lightning and cut off its head. The head still exists in the form of Cabezon Peak, the biggest of the old volcanic necks scattered southeast of Tsoodzil. The monster's dried blood forms the huge fields of lava that spread for miles west of the mountain.

I had planned for years to use the mountain as a setting for a story. It would concern two men. One would be a local fugitive who knew it well and was using its caves, forests, and wilderness of fallen timber as his hiding places; the other a Navajo tribal policeman determined to find him. But when I went there to get a feel for the setting, I found myself thinking instead of the uranium mines that surround the mountain, and the power, wealth, and danger they represented. The book became *People of Darkness*. It had nothing at all to do with hiding places and a lot to do with greed and uranium.

Mount Taylor looks down onto what was the heart of America's uranium country. To the west and north lies the dry plain called (odd as it sounds) Ambrosia Lake. To the east there's the broken mesa country of the Laguna Indian Reservation and an immense hole, the abandoned open pit of the Jackpile mine.

The Ambrosia Lake mines and the Jackpile were America's principal source of uranium during the Cold War years. They made the Laguna tribe relatively affluent for a time and cluttered the old carrot and hay fields with little boom-villages serving the uranium mills.

The mines are closed now—the last one being shut down as this essay was begun. The big, ugly mills where thousands of tons of uranium "yellowcake" were turned out for processing into the enriched metal to fuel nuclear reactors and make bombs are all silent. Some have been abandoned long enough to take on that grown-from-the-earth appearance that ghost towns have. You look at them now—and at the fences converted into gray walls of tumbleweeds and the sand drifting across their roadways—and are reminded that out here man has never been the dominant force.

Anasazi black-on-white bowl.

Oil tanks, basalt formations, and eroded cliffs north of Cuba, New Mexico.

A small sea of grass in northwest New Mexico.

*Above: Navajo homestead on the Big Reservation
with traditional log hogan.
Right: Goat herd at Big Mountain, Arizona.
Following pages: Land of Room Enough and Time.*

T he hogan was a neat octagon of logs built
as the Navajo Way instructed, its single
entrance facing the point of sunrise and a
smoke hole in the center of the roof.

From Dance Hall of the Dead

Windmill surrenders but religion holds on on the Llano Estacado of eastern New Mexico.

A line of winterfat adds a touch of silver to the tan-gray-blue landscape in northern Arizona Navajo country.

R ain loomed over him. It hung over the northeast slopes of
Black Mesa like a wall—illuminated to light gray now and
then by sheet lightning. The smell of it came through the
pickup vents, mixed with the smell of dust. In Chee's desert-
trained nostrils it was heady perfume—the smell of good grazing,
easy water, heavy crops of piñon nuts. The smell of good times, the
smell of Sky Father blessing Mother Earth.

From Skinwalkers

Clouds make more promises than they keep in
desert country. A weather front drifts fruitlessly over
the malpais east of the Zuni Mountains (above), and
a cloud withholds its rain from the cholla, juniper and
grama grass in New Mexico (left).

65

CHACO CANYON: ANCESTORS OF OUR ENEMIES

◆◆◆

If you look north by northeast from Tsoodzil across the detritus of long-gone uranium-mining prosperity scattered throughout the Ambrosia Lake flatlands, you see Chaco Mesa. It's fifty-five crow-flight miles away but looks much closer through the clear dry air. On that mesa, and along both sides of Chaco Wash, stand the remains of man's first organized effort to colonize this harsh, beautiful, and inhospitable landscape. In this unlikely place about a thousand years ago, some of the Anasazis (the name derives from a Navajo phrase that means "ancestors of our enemies") were building what seems to have been the Rome and Mecca of their civilization. Less likely still, they walked away from it about eight hundred years ago, leaving—literally—the dishes on the table.

For as long as I can remember, a casual debate has been underway concerning whether the road to the Chaco Culture National Historical Park should be improved. As it stands, visitors have a choice of two access routes. If they approach from the south via Navajo Route 9, the last twenty miles is dirt, bumpy but passable except when winter snowmelt makes it sticky or summer thundershowers make it slick. If you come down from the north, turning off New Mexico Route 44 at the Blanco Trading Post, you face twenty-six miles of dirt road.

Above: A cholla cactus blooming near Zuni Pueblo.
Left: The work of Anasazi masons resists time against a Chaco Canyon cliff.

*A*ccumulated potsherds provide evidence of "look at it but leave it" courtesy of amateur anthropologists.

I am among those who believe some rough road discourages the idly curious and leaves these remarkable ruins less crowded for those who want to see them badly enough to endure a bit of hardship.

In fact, hardship is part of the mystery that makes Chaco so intriguing to me. You get there by driving through miles of rolling prairie. Technically you are in the San Juan Basin, a circular depression about one hundred miles in diameter with mountain ranges to the north, east, and west and uplifted plateau to the south. The basin is relatively flat, ranging in altitude from a little more than a mile to about 7,500 feet, with precipitation averaging less than eight inches a year (enough to provide a wet weekend on the Gulf Coast). If you are among those who appreciate high desert flora, it's a lovely landscape, covered mostly with dry country grasses—silver, tan, gray, gold, purple, and about any color but green. Here you see buffalo grass and grama, Indian rice grass, bunch grass, and needle grass. There is rabbit brush, snakeweed, desert aster, tumbleweed, and two or three varieties of Jimson weed. But except for cholla cactus and an occasional juniper, there's no sign of fuel wood because there's no sign of water. The rule of nature in the high, dry West is no water, no people. The Anasazis seem to have known how to ignore it even if we don't.

Once you leave the Navajo Eastern Regional Center at Crownpoint behind you, it is thirty-seven miles to Chaco Canyon. Over that distance, you pass one abandoned building and a turnoff road that leads down a hill to a ranch house. That's all.

Scientists assure us that a thousand years ago, when the Anasazi culture was flourishing at Chaco, the climate was much the same: dry, cold winters and hot summers, with scanty precipitation coming mostly from snowstorms or torrential late-summer thunderstorms—poor timing for farmers. Then as now, the bed of Chaco Wash must have carried water only during spring snowmelt and during summer flash floods.

Despite that, surveyors of a forty-three-square-mile area around and including the U.S. Park Service Chaco location turned up 2,220 sites where Anasazis lived and worked. Generation after generation they evolved a civilization and built great stone apartment-

*E*rosion uncovers the pink of iron oxide in the foothills of the Sierra Nacimiento west of Los Alamos.

T hunderheads had merged over the Carrizo range, forming a blue-black wall that extended westward far into Arizona. The afternoon sun lit their tops, already towering high enough to be blowing ice crystals into the jet stream winds.

From Skinwalkers

*A*nasazi pots.

A storm brews off Ojo Redondo Mesa on the Tesuque Indian Reservation.

70

Autumn on the Jicarilla Apache Reservation.

The Rio de los Animas Perdidas (The River of Lost Souls) winds its way
down from the San Juan Wilderness Area.

Basaltic caprock shattered and scattered after the sandstone eroded away from beneath it.

During the eleventh century, the peak Anasazi building period at Chaco, it is estimated that from seventy-five to a hundred thousand trees, principally Ponderosa pine and fir, were cut and carried in to build the great Chaco Canyon apartment-towns. Anthropologists believe they have discovered an Anasazi lumber camp in the mountains of southern Colorado. They believe these people cut timber there and floated the logs southward down towns up and down the wash (Pueblo Bonito, the largest, being four stories tall and includ-ing more than six hundred rooms). They developed what must have been an elaborate religion, established a system of government, practiced art and astronomy, built a network of roads, and domesticated turkeys and dogs. Then, rather abruptly and rather near the peak flowering of their culture, they walked away. Behind them they left their pots, kitchen utensils, bedding, tools for farming, and those odds and ends that make everyday living easier. They also left behind their treasures—jewelry, parrot feathers imported from the jungles a thousand miles south, abalone shell from the Gulf of California, sacred objects used in their ceremonials—and a multitude of unanswered questions.

The most baffling question for fellows like my brother Barney and me, who grew up on a submarginal dryland farm and know arable land when we see it, is why the Chacoans chose the Chaco Mesa country in the first place. From the rim of the mesa above the ruins on the canyon floor you can see at least a hundred miles in every direction. Ninety-five miles to the north, Hesperus Peak, another of the Navajo sacred boundary mountains, rises more than thirteen thousand feet, with Snowstorm Peak and Sliderock Mountain beside it. To the east, it is sixty-five miles to the Jemez Range. South, Tsoodzil juts on the horizon and you see the forested high country of the Continental Divide. West, it is a fifty-mile walk to the Chuska Mountains.

Each of those highland formations is drained by perennial streams that flow even through the driest of summers. Valleys in each of them offer moist, loamy bottom land, game and fish, a wealth of fuel, and convenient shelter. Given the Anasazis' architectural bent, those mountains offered something almost as important as water—big timbers to roof their ceremonial chambers.

A Jemez Reservation juniper bent by a hard life.

the San Juan River to serve as posts and roof beams. But from Pueblo Bonito to the nearest bend in the San Juan is forty-five miles. That's a long way to carry logs, and the Anasazis had neither pack animals nor the wheel. Yet thousands of those logs got to Chaco Canyon somehow, and the nearest alternate source would have been either the Chuska Mountains or Tsoodzil—both at least fifty miles away.

Why didn't the Chacoan people build their great structures beside the rivers? When their descendants resumed the practice of building apartment-towns in the fourteenth and fifteenth centuries, some of them—such as the Hopis, Zunis, and Acomas—stuck to stony dry country. But most moved to the well-watered places. Their new towns arose in the fertile valleys of the Rio Grande drainage.

Obviously, the Chaco people knew the river systems well. Two of their outposts, the Salmon and Aztec ruins, adjoin the San Juan and Animas rivers, respectively, in rich parts of their valleys. In fact, the townsmen of Chaco seem to have been well informed on many fronts. Robert and Florence Lister, who spent much of their lives becoming eminent authorities on the Anasazis, suggest that in the hundred years between 1020 and 1120 the Chacoans became a sort of religious, administrative, and trading hub for much of the widely scattered Anasazi culture. Continuing anthropological studies make it clear that unusual things were happening during that period.

The population around the canyon, more or less stable for five centuries, suddenly burgeoned to as many as six thousand (more than double its traditional level). These people

Restored Anasazi kivas at Mesa Verde.

occupied some four hundred sites, but most of them lived in large apartment-towns concentrated along a nine-mile stretch of the canyon. To the six major structures that existed before 1020, ten more were added. Anasazis from other areas moved in, bringing with them their own building techniques and pottery styles, and the Chacoans themselves began using more sophisticated techniques, including walls of cored masonry that allowed buildings as high as five stories with several hundred rooms. They built, for reasons still unknown, a system of roads even though they had neither pack animals nor carts. They built—for obvious reasons—systems of retaining dams, lined channels, and irrigation ditches to funnel rainwater from the stony mesa tops into their fields in the canyon. They operated both a trading and political system

*F*ormer homestead of a starved-out ranch on Zia Indian land.

*F*ollowing pages: A cloud shadows Enchanted Mesa (center),
where Acoma Indian ancestors were trapped
when an access stairway fell away.

Formations on the Jicarilla Reservation let the imagination play its games.

that allowed for the allocation of labor; they probably developed a merchant class, certainly developed a religious hierarchy, and imported goods from as far away as the tropics of Central America and the Pacific Coast. And then they went away and left it all behind.

The quickest way for me to get to Chaco is via Interstate 40 to Thoreau, then northward through the Navajo eastern administrative center at Crownpoint. The most pleasant way is to take New Mexico Highway 44 to Cuba. At that little town you turn onto the narrow asphalt of Route 197, which makes its bumpy way seventy-six miles through the "Checkerboard Reservation," which is partly reserved Navajo land, partly private land, partly federal "public domain" land, partly Navajo "allotment land," and mostly vacant. Those unused to desert country maps would expect to be

Deer at Mesa Verde seem to know man is no longer dreadful here.

driving through a series of small towns—Penistaja, Navajo Mission, Torreon, Pueblo Alto, Pueblo Pintado and, finally, White Horse Lake. But Penistaja is merely the point where a dirt road connects with Route 197, Navajo Mission is a church and two or three little buildings about two miles off the highway, Torreon is a trading post which wasn't open the last time I drove by, and Pueblo Alto and Pueblo Pintado are Anasazi ruins abandoned centuries ago and now the sites, respectively, of a little store and a day school. White Horse Lake is a trading post with two gasoline pumps; it sometimes closes early. The vehicle I drive has a twenty-two-gallon gasoline tank, and I always make sure it's full when I head into the empty corners.

Any approach to Chaco involves a trip through miles of beautiful desolation—an explicit reminder that Chaco Mesa country provides sustenance for only a few dozen Navajo sheep

Anasazi woven pot rest.

*G*roundsel in bloom.

herders and even fewer white ranchers. In this respect, the Route 197 approach is a bit better than the others. It offers one of America's best chances to drive seventy-five miles of pavement without seeing another human—with the final twenty miles of dirt capping off the sensation. By the time I cross the last ridge and look down into the great grassy basin drained by Chaco Wash, the big question has risen again in my mind. Why did they choose this inhospitable site? How could six thousand people, or even a thousand, possibly stay alive in this place?

The U.S. Park Service provides guided tours of the ruins, but it also respects the yearnings of some of us to see them alone and at our own pace. In the off-season it's possible to visit even the most popular and impressive sites—Pueblo Bonito, for example, or Casa Rinconada, that strange Chacoan version of Saint Peter's Cathedral—with no company other than one's thoughts. And it seems that neither Pueblo Bonito nor Casa Rinconada can fail to provoke thought in anyone interested in peering down the dark road humanity has traveled.

I suspect I am partial to Pueblo Bonito because I am fond of ironies and oddities, and the immense slab of sandstone that split off the cliff of Chaco Mesa and crushed the back wall of this ruin fascinates me. The slab called Threatening Rock was about one hundred feet tall, weighed thirty thousand tons, and was leaning over the building when it was first discovered by white people. Obviously, it had been leaning since the eleventh century, because the Bonitians then in residence built buttresses and used pine log props to help support it. The U.S. Park Service called in modern engineers. They disapproved of the Anasazi preservation methods and recommended that the debris filling the slot between slab and cliff be removed. This was done. At 4:32 P.M. on January 21, 1941, Threatening Rock fell with a concussion heard for miles, smashing the best and highest portion of Bonito's back wall and destroying sixty-five rooms. (Some local Navajos do not blame the disaster on the declining quality of engineering skills down the centuries. Instead, they say anthropologists climbed Fajada Butte, a tower of sandstone that overlooks the canyon, thereby irritating a witch long known to live there. In retaliation the witch toppled Threatening Rock.)

Before this mishap, Neil M. Judd had spent years studying and excavating Pueblo Bonito for the National Geographic Society and the National Museum of Natural History. He concluded that at its zenith between the tenth and eleventh centuries, this apartment-town was four stories tall, had 651 rooms, and housed about one thousand people. In it, side by side and in apparent peace, lived two diverse cultures. Judd called them Old Bonitians and

The sandstone rim of Jemez Mesa on the Jemez Reservation.

T he quirky wind generated by the thunderstorms' great updrafts bounced a tumbleweed across the unpaved clinic parking lot just as he pulled his truck to stop.

From Skinwalkers

◆◆◆

Sheep pen sans sheep east of Tucumcari, New Mexico.

Late Bonitians. The latter arrived after the former had already built an arch-shaped structure. They expanded and remodeled it, using masonry techniques allowing higher walls, changing its shape from an open C to a closed D, digging new kivas in the courtyard and building more of these little chapels into existing rooms. There were other changes, too. Windows were made smaller, interior doorway sizes were decreased, outside access ways were reduced to a single door, and then even that was filled in, leaving access by ladders only. Defensive measures, obviously. But measures against what? Anthropologists have found no evidence of warfare in Chaco.

Doorways once used by Anasazi families at Mesa Verde.

You can walk through those Bonito rooms today, ducking through the low doorways that connect them, wondering about such things, wondering why these small people built such high ceilings, staring through the narrow windows at the same arid, stony landscape that must have been the despair of generation after generation of Anasazi farmers.

Across Chaco Wash (totally dry this winter afternoon) and up the slope, Casa Rinconada looks down on this abandoned dwelling. It seems to have been an intercommunity religious center—certainly it is large enough. Its central feature is a great kiva (the chapel has become a church), sixty-three feet in diameter, dug into the shale of the hillside with masonry walls rising around it. Antechambers were built on two sides of it. One, perhaps a dressing room for priests or performers, was linked to the kiva floor by a tunnel from which one could emerge behind what was probably a screen. On the kiva floor itself are a firebox, bench seating, stone vaults, the bases for four massive timbers that supported the roof, and, around the walls, thirty-four open niches of unguessable purpose.

Casa Rinconada is open to the sky now, the timbers of its roof having long since rotted away. On this breezy winter day the cold air whips under your pant legs and rolls a tumbleweed along the slope below and causes you to give some credence to the most widely accepted theory of why this place was abandoned: The eleventh century population boom produced more people than the valley could feed. Drought worsened conditions and famine produced social stress. People moved out looking for better places to the south.

But every logical answer at Chaco seems to remind you of another question. What happened to the dead they left behind? Anasazi town dwellers usually dug their graves

Nothing much but thistles and saltbush now grows where this Anasazi town once thrived beside Chaco Mesa.

The shadow of Fajada Butte stretched all the way across Chaco Wash now. Outside the shadow, the yellow of the cottonwood along the dry streambed glittered in the sun. They were the only trees in a tan-gray-silver universe of grass. Where had they found their firewood, Leaphorn wondered, the vanished thousands of Old Ones who built these huge stone apartments? The anthropologists thought they'd carried the roof beams fifty miles on their shoulders from forests on Mount Taylor and the Chuskas—an incredible feat. But how did they boil their corn, roast venison, cure their pottery, and warm themselves in winter?

From A Thief of Time

◆◆◆

*A*nasazi handled bowl.

*T*he ruins of an Anasazi apartment, the Chaco Canyon cliffs, and the inevitable question—why here?

against the walls of inner rooms, making them easy to find. But thorough excavations of Pueblo Bonito, Cheto Ketl, Pueblo Alto, and Pueblo del Arroyo, four major towns where thousands of people had lived generation after generation, yielded a total of only 121 burials—a tiny fraction of what would be expected. Searches for mass burial sites revealed nothing. Cremation? Two fire pits large enough for that purpose were located, but the residue in neither showed any trace of human bone fragments or bone ash.

And you remember what scientists such as Judd, the Listers, Dabney Ford, and scores of others have been digging out of this place for half a century: Under a collapsed ceiling a collection of carved, painted figures, some birdlike, some abstract, which might have been used in a religious ceremony. Under a stone slab covering a cavity in a floor thousands of carved turquoise beads. In another floor cache an elaborate necklace made up of four strands on which twenty-five hundred turquoise beads were strung. Elsewhere, flutes, pipes, macaw feathers, tools, jewelry, and decorated pottery—the sort of items that must have been family treasures. Cached in a crevice between rocks a farmer's carefully made planting sticks and his tools to cut weeds and cultivate the ground.

Why were the luxury items left behind?

But being raised a dryland farm boy, I turn from thoughts of jewelry and macaw feathers to that planting stick and weeding tools left behind the rock. What could have kept that farmer from coming back for them?

*A*nasazi pitchers.

*B*lack-eyed Susans and summer
take over a Navajo corn field.

Behind him, above the red sandstone wall of the mesa, a skyscape of feathery cirrus clouds stretched southward toward Mexico. To the west over the Painted Desert, they were flushed with the afterglow of sunset. To the north this reflected light colored the cliffs of the Zuñi Buttes a delicate rose.

From Dance Hall of the Dead

◆ ◆ ◆

Snakeweed, Mormon tea, a little sage, and a few tough clumps of gramma grass make poor grazing on the Navajo Reservation.

93

Erosion forms its own abstract art in a sandstone cliff.

*Snakeweed, asters, rabbitbrush, saltbush, and
juniper south of Grants, New Mexico.
Following pages: A butte cut into an arc by erosion
on the north side of the Navajo Reservation.*

CANYON DE CHELLY

O n the map mounted on the wall above my word processor, Canyon de Chelly resembles the track a bird might leave in the mud. The heel mark is the canyon mouth, its place of exit from Defiance Plateau down into Chinle Valley. The toes form its three major branches—Canyon de Chelly itself in the center cutting some twenty-five miles eastward into the plateau, Massacre Canyon extending twenty miles to the northeast, and Monument Canyon angling southeastward. On that map Canyon de Chelly seems relatively insignificant, a medium-sized gorge (by Rocky Mountain standards) sharing the territory with the immense Grand Canyon and the spectacular slot through which the Little Colorado River drains. Nor does de Chelly make much of an impression when you drive to its mouth from the nearby Navajo town of Chinle, Arizona. While its flat, sandy bottom is almost three hundred yards wide, the cliffs that wall it in at this point rise only about thirty feet. In terms of geology or hydrology, it seems to be just another of those washes that drain snowmelt and summer rains from the Chuska Mountains.

But in terms of history and matters of the human spirit, Canyon de Chelly is much more special than that. Traditional Navajos know it from their mythic poetry as the living place

Above: Flowers in red shale on the Navajo Reservation.
Left: Anasazi storage structures along Chinle Wash.

of Yeibichai, the Talking God who, as the maternal grandfather in their pantheon of spirits, serves as spokesman for God himself. They know it as the place from which Changing Woman, the law-giver of their theology, left this Earth Surface World to join her lover, the Sun. As clan headman Barboncito told General Sherman during the negotiations of the treaty that brought the Navajos home from interment at Bosque Redondo, the canyon is "the very heart of our country."

But the canyon was occupied long before the Navajos arrived. With some peculiar gaps, a sequence of civilizations has lived in it for two thousand years. The objects these occupants left behind make it a unique outdoor museum of the evolution of cultures. And then there is its beauty—the shapes and colors that many millennia of erosion have produced in its cliffs. For a friend of mine, and probably for thousands of others, there is something about it that's harder to define.

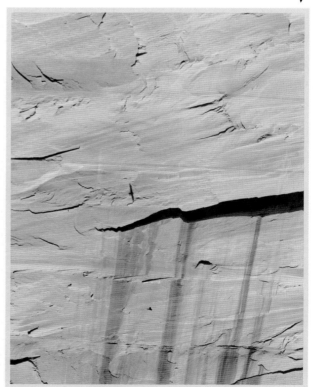

A raven's shadow on the pink sandstone cliffs near Chinle.

I last saw this friend about five years ago. She was en route from her home in Washington to the Navajo Reservation and we met for lunch. Her cigarette cough had become more than that. Her doctor had shown her the X rays and told her that smoking had caused cancer in both lungs. An operation would be futile. She must measure her life in months now, and she intended to use them well. First of all, she would revisit Canyon de Chelly.

"A special place," she said, and I agreed. But why? To answer that, she recounted the first time she had seen the place. She'd been assigned to Gallup by the federal bureau for which she worked, and someone suggested she visit that national monument. She had driven out on one of those hot August days when the thunderclouds build in the sky but the air is still too dry for rain. She had stopped at the monument headquarters, decided against joining the guided tour offered there, and took the long climb down from the rim on the trail leading to White House Ruins. She had splashed through the cold, shallow water of Chinle Wash to stand in the shade under that ancient Anasazi cliff house.

Perhaps being barefooted on the wet sand had produced childhood memories, she said. Perhaps it was because she had seen so many photographs of that spectacular spot. Whatever

I n the narrow stone alcove, Anasazi families had built a two-story dwelling probably big enough for thirty people. Above it, in another alcove so hidden that they wouldn't have noticed it had Eddie not wondered where an evening bat flight was coming from, the Anasazi had built a little stone fort reachable only by a precarious set of hand- and footholds.

From A Thief of Time

◆◆◆

Left: Canyon de Chelly with Anasazi ruins. Navajo headman Barboncito called the canyon "the very heart of our country." Below: Tsaile Creek hides under a Canyon del Muerto cliff.

Navajo cattle wading in Chinle Wash.

caused it, she had felt an overpowering sense of having been there before; of knowing what would be around the next corner before she looked; of this first visit being somehow a return to a place important to her.

"Something to do with the stillness, maybe; with climbing down into all that silence, with the cliffs shutting everything out, with knowing that in another time there was another civilization down here," she said. Or perhaps it was because the cliffs are so overpowering that they made her feel tiny and not in control. Or perhaps this sense of being diminished by the scale of things caused her imagination to work in an unusual way.

In my own case, all these factors seem to be involved. Certainly that canyon has caused my imagination to work. There one Septem-

A view between Canyon de Chelly cliffs.

ber day a long time ago the thought came to me that grew into a book I named *Enemy Way*. (Harper & Row renamed it *The Blessing Way*.) It was a perfectly natural notion considering the setting. What would one do if caught in this canyon? What if the way out downstream was barred and someone was hunting him? Where I stood on the damp sand the cliffs towered over me, almost vertical and utterly unclimbable. Common sense and a boyhood that included exploring creeks told me there would be ways out. But how could I find one? How could one escape this trap?

Historically, the canyon has indeed been a trap. In 1805 a Lieutenant Antonio Narbona and his Mexican troops slaughtered Navajo refugees there, giving both this branch of the canyon and Massacre Cave their names. In the bitter winter of 1863, Colonel Kit Carson's troops cornered hundreds of Navajos here and captured them in the climactic action that broke the tribe's resistance to white domination. There is some reason to believe that the Anasazis who built their stone dwellings in the canyon walls may also have been caught here in a losing battle with invaders. Skulls apparently broken with stone axes have been found, and some thousand-year-old pictographs seem to represent men armed with throwing sticks being attacked by men shooting arrows from bows—a deadly weapon the Anasazis never developed.

If the canyon was a trap, then water was the bait. At the canyon mouth, where Chinle Wash is as wide as three football fields and the sand is seventy feet deep, the surface of the

Following pages: The Navajo name for this lifeless expanse of multicolored desolation translates to "Beautiful Valley."

The moon had risen just above the cliff behind her. Out on the packed sand of the wash bottom the shadow of the walker made a strange elongated shape. Sometimes it suggested a heron, sometimes one of those stick-figure forms of an Anasazi pictograph. An animated pictograph, its arms moving rhythmically as the moon shadow drifted across the sand. Sometimes, when the goat trail bent and put the walker's profile against the moon, the shadow became Kokopelli himself. The backpack formed the spirit's grotesque hump, the walking stick Kokopelli's crooked flute. Seen from above, the shadow would have made a Navajo believe that the great yei northern clans called Watersprinkler had taken visible form. If an Anasazi had risen from his thousand-year grave in the trash heap under the cliffs ruins here, he would have seen the Humpbacked Flute Player, the rowdy god of fertility of his lost people. But the shadow was only the shape of Dr. Eleanor Friedman-Bernal blocking out the light of an October moon. . . .

The moon lit only a part of the wall and the slanting light made it difficult to see, but she stopped to inspect it. In this light, the tapered, huge-shouldered shape of the mystic Anasazi shaman lost its color and became merely a dark form. Above it a clutter of shapes danced, stick figures, abstractions: the inevitable Kokopelli, his humped shape bent, his flute pointed almost at the ground; a heron flying; a heron standing; the zigzag band of pigment representing a snake. Then she noticed the horse. . . .

Wherever you found him—and you found him everywhere these vanished people carved, and painted, their spirits into the cliffs of the Southwest—Kokopelli looked about the same. His humpbacked figure was supported by stick legs. Stick arms held a straight line to his tiny round head, making him seem to be playing a clarinet. The flute might be pointed down, or ahead. Otherwise there was little variation in how he was depicted. Except here. Here Kokopelli was lying on his back, flute pointed skyward. "At last," Eddie had said. "You have found Kokopelli's home. This is where he sleeps.". . .

From A Thief of Time

◆◆◆

A graceful version of Kokopelli plays
his flute in Chinle Wash.

streambed will sometimes be dry between the end of snow runoff and summer rains. But even then you can reach water by digging for it. And in years of heavy snows or early "monsoon" season, the wash will carry a live stream far out into the Chinle Valley all summer long. In a landscape where water was scarce, every primitive nomad must have known this. They would also have known that even in the driest times fresh water could be found by walking up the canyons of either Chinle Wash or Tsaile Creek. Even in midwinter, springs seeping into their narrow upper canyons keep them fed with cold, clear water.

This water seems to have first sustained a permanent population of humans a bit before the time of Christ—a civilization the anthropologists call the Basketmakers. Only a few families lived here—a peak population of perhaps two hundred—and they seemed to have clustered near where Monument Canyon empties into Canyon de Chelly and halfway up Canyon del Muerto. They grew corn in the same fields Navajos farm today and kept their surplus along with grass seeds, gourds, and other produce in storage cysts scooped out of the sandstone under overhanging cliffs. In such cysts at Mummy Cave up Canyon del Muerto, anthropologists also found burial sites—the bodies tied in fetal positions and wrapped in deerskin, or in blankets sewn of rabbit fur or woven from yucca fibers. Their valuables were left with the bodies—bone flutes, tobacco pipes, carved ornaments, digging sticks, and weapons. The natural preservation of the bodies in this dry climate was so total that anthropologists can describe their hairstyles. (The women wore short bangs, and the men favored long braids with the hair cut short at the crown into a monklike tonsure.)

For about four hundred years, this tiny canyon-bottom civilization seems to have existed with scant evolution. The anthropologists, who notice even minuscule cultural changes, draw lines dividing twelve hundred years of prehistoric humanity in the canyon. The Basketmakers become Modified Basketmakers, then Developmental Pueblo, and finally

Hopi coiled basket.

An Anasazi storage structure above Chinle.

A view up Canyon de Chelly.

Moody horses waiting in Canyon de Chelly.

*C*ottonwoods in Canyon de Chelly.

Great Pueblo people. There the chart ends. Told another way, little storage cysts originally cut into the stone and then walled with other stones gradually grew in size and developed into pit houses. The oldest roof beam found on such a structure came from a tree cut in A.D. 480. Another five hundred years would pass (equivalent to the time between Columbus' "discovery" of America and 1992) before the first of the canyon's stone-walled cliff dwellings was built. The Basketmakers had become the civilization we call Anasazi.

In the main canyon alone, the ruins of sixty-seven of these stone structures have been found and dated. By the twelfth or thirteenth century, the population in the canyon reached a high estimated at eight hundred. We know they were small people with a life expectancy of only about forty years and that they were part of the same complex civilization that flourished at Chaco Canyon, Mesa Verde, and throughout the Colorado Plateau. Judging from what clues remain, the canyon, in its Anasazi age, received a final influx of immigrants in the middle of the thirteenth century—probably families from the suddenly deserted cliff dwellings at Mesa Verde. In 1264 the last log was cut somewhere on the plateau above to become a beam in an Anasazi structure.

Then silence descended on the canyon. Everyone went away. Civilization ended between the great red cliffs.

The Navajos, who traditionally give meaning to life's mysteries in pictures and poetry, have their explanation of what happened to the Anasazis. It goes like this:

The *anaasa'zi* (or "ancestors of the enemy people") were especially blessed by God, having received the gift of corn and the knowledge of architecture, pottery, animal domestication, and powerful religious ceremonials to keep their life easy and content. In return, they were expected to live within the rules. After many generations, these people became softened by the easy life and grew lazy. Their culture decayed. Incest was practiced, and illnesses and birth defects became common. To offset this effect they began misusing the Wind Way, a ceremonial given them (and to the Navajos, who still use it) to restore harmony of mind and spirit. Instead of using it as a cure, they used it as a preventive, so they could continue an evil life without ill effects. Four times the Holy People appeared and warned them. The warnings were ignored. Then a catastrophic flaming whirlwind swept down the canyon, blowing away the Anasazis.

Red-roofed Navajo hogan on the floor of Canyon del Muerto.

That legend explains why the remains of so few humans are found in the canyon, and accounts for the dark sootlike stains of "desert varnish" that streak the canyon walls. The Navajo clans who occupy the original Dinetah homeland of the tribe in New Mexico offer a different version. They say that the Holy People who would later create the Navajos found that the great apartment-towns at Chaco were occupied by Anasazis who had bet and lost everything they owned, even their freedom, in a dice game with a magician called Never Loses. Now the Anasazis lived as his slaves. Never Loses had also won an object coveted by the Sun. To regain this object for the Sun, the Holy People challenged Never Loses to a series of gambling games. By some shrewd cheating they won freedom for the Anasazis and all that Never Loses possessed, including Never Loses himself. A great wind thereupon picked up the magician gambler and carried him away to Mexico. Unfortunately for the Anasazis, they too were blown away.

Anthropologists have their own theory, with much supporting evidence. They hold that these people simply migrated to reappear eventually, settling the Hopi villages and developing the Pueblo Indian cultures of the Rio Grande valley and western New Mexico. Whatever happened, wherever they went, Anasazi ghosts still haunt this silent canyon.

That very last timber cut in 1264 became a roof beam in a three-story structure we call The Tower. It perches high on the east cliff of Canyon del Muerto, not far from Mummy Cave, on a shelf of sandstone which connects two alcoves. The first time I saw it was on a late afternoon with the slanting sunlight illuminating the top of the cliff above it. Seen from the premature twilight of the canyon depth, the walls of the ruins seemed to glow. Absolute silence. A situation that stirs the imagination.

The Tower was built just at the time the great cliff houses at Mesa Verde were abandoned. Its builders used the masonry techniques characteristic of Mesa Verde, and the pottery found in it was Mesa Verde pottery. Thus you conclude that its builders were refugees. But from what? Perhaps from starvation. About then an epic drought had stunted tree growth on the Colorado Plateau for twenty years. But it seems obvious that The Tower was situated and built as a fortress. Were these people fleeing from invaders? Had Ute and Paiute nomads, users of the bow, moved into Anasazi territory? We know that several of the mummified bodies found inside the structure seem to have died violently. Another, at the Ts'e-ta'a structure built about the same time, had his skull fractured by a stone ax. Had there been war, then, in this peaceful place?

You lean against the cool cliff and let your imagination travel in time. Perhaps you imagine warfare—barbarians scrambling up that steep slope under the walls to slaughter exhausted defenders. Perhaps you see the last family leaving, small people, lean from famine, hurrying, leaving behind many things they must have valued, carrying only a few baskets and pots and ceremonial objects of their religion. Going where?

Cliff dwellings in Canyon de Chelly.
Following pages: Chinle Wash emerging from the
mouth of Canyon de Chelly.

Perhaps they went west. Hopi mythology tells us that by the fourteenth century their Bear Clan had already established the villages of Shongopovi and Oraibi at the south end of Black Mesa. The story of the migrations of the Hopi clans fits neatly into this theory. In Hopi tradition the ruins in this canyon, as well as those at Mesa Verde, Keet Seel, Salmon, Chaco, Casa Grande, and the others scattered across the desert west, are merely footprints left behind by their various clans wandering toward their destiny on the Hopi mesas, the "Middle Place" of the universe.

Whatever happened, wherever these Anasazis went, Canyon de Chelly was left empty for centuries. From about 1300 to about 1750, the land walled in by these great cliffs seems to have been occupied only by its ghosts.

Even now the canyon is almost empty in the winter season. Most of the four or five hundred Navajos who plant the cornfields and tend the goat herds in the canyon bottom during the summer move out about the time snow comes. Winters are cold at the six-thousand-foot altitude of Defiance Plateau. Frigid air sinking to the canyon bottom makes the cold bitter there, and the winter sun, low on the southern horizon, doesn't reach in with its heat. But if you enjoy lonely silence, winter afternoons are a time to come.

Down through the years I have developed my own ritual for such visits. I drive north from Window Rock, following Navajo Route 12 along the west slope of the Chuskas, then circling back on Navajo 64 along the north rim. I stop at the Mummy Cave overlook and, if there's plenty of time, stop again to do some loitering at the Antelope House and Ledge House sites.

Wildflowers.

Seen from the rim, the canyon is awe-inspiring. Even the larger ruins seem too trivial to notice, overpowered by the vastness. But when you are on the surface below, the atmosphere is different. The cliffs close you into a very small place, with the outside world excluded. You exist in the bottom of a bottle. At locations such as Standing Cow Ruin, where reminders of man's efforts to survive and evolve surround you, this sense of human fragility and futility can be overwhelming.

Standing Cow Ruin in Canyon del Muerto is one of the largest in the eighty-four-thousand-acre Canyon de Chelly National Monument. Here the Anasazis built sixty rooms for living and storage and three kivas for their ceremonials. Its walls enclose an area forty feet wide and four hundred feet long, and the cliffs for hundreds of yards up and down the

*T*he window that gives Window Rock its name.

*F*ollowing pages: In this Navajo pictograph on a cliff of
Canyon del Muerto, the dragoons of Lieutenant Antonio
Narbona ride toward the murderous destiny that gave
both the canyon and Massacre Cave their names.

Grazing is where you find it between Crystal and Sheep Springs in the Chuska Mountains.

canyon are a gallery of pictographs. The art and graffiti of more than a thousand years is represented here, from hand prints and abstractions left by Basketmakers to Navajo recordings of their encounters with the Mexican soldiers and Kit Carson's troopers. Within the space of a mile you can puzzle over stylized humanoid figures with looped arms and bird-like feet, figures holding hands, displaying cryptic objects, humans with horns, and humans with their torsos decorated with handprints. Mixed with all these are much later and much cruder paintings of the pueblo builders—stick figures, concentric circles (which a Hopi friend tells me represent the mythic migrations of the Hopi clans), a humpbacked archer, armless humanoid shapes, depictions of snakes and designs that might be the Hopi symbol for rain clouds. A few yards away, and perhaps a thousand years distant in time, is a life-sized Navajo representation of the standing cow that gives the ruins its name.

Up the cliff, pale against the dark red sandstone, is one of the West's most remarkable pictographs. Lieutenant Narbona and his cavalry are drawn in a line across the stone. They wear the broad-brimmed hats of Mexican cavalry, carry muskets, and ride their stick-legged horses toward their terrible victory.

I doubt if any veteran of ground combat in any war could walk up the packed sand of Canyon del Muerto without respecting the courage of that Mexican lieutenant, if not the brutality of the campaign. Narbona had been sent up from Chihuahua in command of 303 soldiers to help New Mexico militiamen fight the Navajos. Legend held that this canyon was the Navajo fortress. Riding into it, even armed with muskets against a foe armed only with bows and lances, must have seemed like riding into the jaws of death.

In his laconic report to the governor, Narbona stated that his force had suffered one dead and sixty-four wounded and had also lost eighty-five of its horses. He reported ninety warriors and twenty-five women and children killed, and three warriors and thirty-two women and children captured. He told the governor that the Navajos' hope of making themselves invincible in the canyon was "not without reason." "I cannot help but make

A Navajo homestead in Canyon de Chelly.

known to your Lordship as doing my duty and without exaggeration, that if in the future it were necessary to attack it again, it would be indispensable that it be done with a greater number of people than those who accompanied me, and that they take a larger supply of ammunition, for that which I brought with me from my Province amounted to more than 10,000 cartridges and in order to get out of the canyon I was obliged to use up most of them."

One sees a different battle through Navajo tribal memory. It tells of families trapped in the canyon when the Mexican troopers swept into the mouth of Chinle Wash, of Navajo braves shooting their arrows from the rocks and being shot down by musket fire, and of old men, women, and children climbing to a high cave some ten miles upstream from the mouth of Canyon del Muerto—a cave in which they had previously hidden from Ute raiders. This sanctuary is about six hundred feet above the canyon floor and some two hundred feet below the rim. Today, and probably then as well, the only access to it is across a narrow ledge. Even this route requires using precarious finger- and toeholds cut into the sandstone.

In one version of this tragedy, a jealous Navajo man betrayed the hiding place to the Mexicans. Another legend has it that a Navajo woman shouted her defiance at the invaders. We know only that the Mexicans managed to climb to where they could shoot into the cave, because its roof and walls are pockmarked by the impact of hundreds of musket balls. The floor of the cave is littered with bones, many of them children's. Navajos call the cave Two Fell Over, the two being a Navajo woman and a Mexican soldier upon whom she sprang, plunging them both six hundred feet down the cliff to their deaths.

With their traditional respect for (and aversion to) the remains of the dead, the Navajos have left the cave alone. But white looters have stolen most of the skulls.

After the canyon became United States territory it was the scene of a series of skirmishes and scouting expeditions—based on the persistent belief that the Navajos had built some sort of a fortress in its vastness. In 1849 Lieutenant Colonel John Washington, a totally black-hearted scoundrel, crossed the Chuska Mountains with a force of five hundred men and a battery of artillery. He explored the canyon complex and found no fortress, but provided a detailed description of its wonders. Two years later, another battalion of troops and artillery invaded the canyon only to be chased out by the Navajos after a scuffle. In 1859 Colonel Dixon Miles led a calvary raid down into Monument Canyon, stealing sheep and killing several Navajos. Finally the role of the place as stronghold for the tribe and arena for war came to an end.

From the beginning of its relations with the Navajos, the United States followed a policy of allowing whites to push into Navajo grazing land, invading Navajo territory whenever the tribe tried to defend its homeland, and then negotiating a treaty. In these treaties, the United States would promise that if the Navajos would stop resisting the land grab and return cattle

Pick your shade of pink from Canyon de Chelly cliffs.

126

A bove and beyond the railroad, beyond the clutter of east Gallup, the red cliffs of Mesa de los Lobos rose—their redness diminished a little by the blue haze of distance, and above them was the gray-green shape of the high country of the Navajo border-lands, where the Big Reservation faded into Checkboard Reservation. For Joe Leaphorn, raised not fifty miles north of this bed in the grass country near Two Gray Hills, it was the landscape of his childhood. But now he looked at the scene without thinking about it.

From Skinwalkers

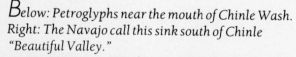

*Below: Petroglyphs near the mouth of Chinle Wash.
Right: The Navajo call this sink south of Chinle "Beautiful Valley."*

that whites always claimed had been stolen, the United States would return captured Navajo children who had been sold into slavery (the price in the Santa Fe market was about $90 a child) and leave the tribe in peace. Upon agreeing to the treaty, the Navajos would deliver a herd of horses and a flock of sheep, ask for the return of their sons and daughters, and be told that this wasn't possible because the captives had become Christians. (To protect their investments, slave buyers adopted the policy of baptizing Navajos promptly after their purchase.) The aforementioned Colonel Washington seems to have refined the process by not even bothering to put copies of treaties on file.

Efficient as this aggression came to be, Territorial Governor James B. Carlton decided to apply a "final solution." Carlton believed

Summer at the foot of Tsaile Mesa on the Navajo Reservation.

that gold could be found in the Chuskas and points west if the Navajos could be eliminated. He named Colonel Carson to command an expedition made up of U.S. regulars, militia, and allies recruited from the Pueblo tribes and the Utes—whom Carson encouraged by promising that they could keep as slaves all the Navajos they could capture. Carson's plan was to harass the Navajos throughout the summer, burning their fields, killing their flocks, stealing their horses, and killing and capturing as many of them as possible. When winter came, cold and starvation would finish the job. The plan worked. By the end of 1863, bands of starving Navajos began surrendering. Then, on January 11, two columns of Carson's troops rode through deep snow into the canyon, invading Canyon del Muerto from the east and the main canyon from its mouth. Navajo resistance was ineffective. When the columns combined, the trickle of surrendering Navajos became a flood. The white men held Tsegi, the place where the spirits lived. Navajo independence was snuffed out forever.

A detachment of troops returned the following summer, burned Navajo hogans, chopped down the peach trees (some five thousand of them) for which the canyon had been known, and captured Barboncito, one of the most respected of the clan headmen. More than eight thousand Navajos were herded eastward into the dismal Bosque Redondo Reservation on the Pecos River. What was left of the tribe was scattered into remote hideouts as distant as Utah. The great complex of canyons was empty again.

Dry Wash waiting for rain in the Kletha Valley, Arizona.

I have a weakness (already confessed) for empty places. Even in its busiest summer season, when Navajo guides are bringing tourists from park headquarters in the required four-wheel-drive vehicles, when canyon-bottom farmers are working their fields, and when herders are moving their flocks, it's still easy enough to find silence and solitude. But if you share my taste for isolation, late autumn or early spring are ideal times to visit. I like to climb down from the rim to White House Ruins, take off my shoes and socks, as my friend did, and splash through the shallow water to the cottonwoods under the cliff dwelling. The sandstone cliffs soaring toward the sky make the ruins seem as small as a dollhouse. And up and down the stream, painted on the tough dark deposits of desert varnish that stain the sandstone, are the pictographs—the work of Basketmaker, Anasazi, Hopi, and Navajo. You wander along the cliffs, finding abstractions, snakes, birds, men with the feet of birds, shaman figures, clan symbols, rows of dots and circled dots, the familiar humpbacked shape of Kokopelli playing his flute, a frog, a large man with arms raised in supplication, a mountain goat impaled by a lance.

I think these are messages left for us that we have forgotten how to read. The cliffs remind me of how little space I occupy; the pictographs, of how little time.

Navajo Ganado Red rug.

Saltbush, snakeweed and bunchgrass soften the malpais lava south of Grants. In the background, Mesa de los Vocao and Mesa de los Toros.

Leaphorn stopped the carryall, turned off the ignition and listened to it coming. The sun slanted into the falling water, creating a gaudy double rainbow which seemed to move steadily toward him, narrowing its arch as it came in accordance with rainbow optics. There was sound now, the muted approaching roar of billions of particles of ice and water striking stone. The first huge drop struck the roof of Leaphorn's carryall. Plong! Plong-plong! And a torrent of rain and hail swept over the vehicle. The screen of falling water dimmed the landscape for a moment, the droplets reflecting the sun like a rhinestone curtain. And then the light was drowned. Leaphorn sat, engulfed in sound. He glanced at his watch, and waited, enjoying the storm as he enjoyed all things right and natural—not thinking for the moment about any of the unnatural affairs that involved him. He put aside the sense of urgency that had brought him down this wagon track much faster than it could wisely be driven. It took a fraction over seven minutes for the storm to pass Leaphorn's carryall.

From Listening Woman

◆◆◆

*R*ain bearing down on the Defiance Plateau.

THE SAN JUAN:
CUT-STONE COUNTRY

◆◆◆

An erudite friend once contended that I was like Miniver Cheevy, Edward Arlington Robinson's "child of scorn," who was born in the wrong season. Just as Miniver yearned for the olden days of chivalry, I longed to live when the multiplying process begun by Adam and Eve was in its earliest stages and it was harder to find fellow humans than it is today to avoid them.

The Anasazis, at least some of them, seem to have been afflicted with the same attitude. While you find their traces just about everywhere in this stony part of the world, remarkably often you find signs of them in locations chosen for reasons that seem purely misanthropic. They seemed to seek out-of-the-way places where there was no risk of meeting other humans.

West of Bluff, Utah, on a stony ridge a half mile from the San Juan River, you notice (once you have learned to notice such things) a slight hump under the thin growth of snakeweed and needle grass. If you follow it, it becomes an almost perfect circle perhaps fifteen feet across. Nature rarely creates such geometry. It must be the top of a kiva wall. Scattered traces of other structures—reduced by a thousand winters to barely noticeable disturbances of the surface, confirm it. A little band of Anasazis once occupied this ridge. Again, the inevitable

Above: Hard times south of Durango beside the Animas River.
Left: Canyon Sin Nombre on the Navajo Reservation in northern Arizona.

Why Bluff, Utah, is called Bluff.

question. Why live in this inconvenient place with the whole world to pick from?

Below, the San Juan meanders through a valley green with cottonwoods, willows, Russian olive, and tamarack. It offers water, fuel, shelter, game, fish, nuts, and berries. This ridge offers only hard labor, an hour's hard climb down to get a drink of water, stony ground, a blistering high-country sun in the summer, and no shelter from the bitter winter wind. The only plus is a spectacular view. Unless, of course, you like to be alone.

This stony circle is on Tank Mesa, between Bluff and Mexican Hat in southern Utah. I was first there in late summer. The time that desert dwellers call their monsoon season had not quite ended. A thunderhead was building to the north over the ragged ramparts of the aptly named Comb Ridge. The place was surrounded by other incipient storms—to the south over the empty sandstone wilderness of the Nokaito Bench, to the west over the village of Bluff, and over Navajo Mountain seventy miles to the east. This is red, tan, pink, and blue country, the colors of sandstone, granite, slate, and, beyond the incredible clouds, the navy blue high-altitude sky. But except for a narrow band along the river no green was visible. Beautiful, yes. But green is the color of life—the color that means food and water. Hard country, this strip of southern Utah along the Navajo Reservation border. Awesome, but not hospitable. Why did it attract the Anasazi?

Until shallow oil was discovered in the Aneth basin, white men saw little to draw them into this hard rock country, and they always had trouble enduring here. Bluff, for example, exists only because the Mormon leader Brigham Young felt he needed an outpost on the San Juan to protect Mormon country from invasion by hostile easterners.

High up the slope above the kiva on Tank Mesa you can find remains of the road these settlers cut into the sandstone to get their wagons across Comb Ridge. Even if you are unburdened, it's a tough climb. It is almost impossible to imagine the labor and hardships of those who dragged their wagons over this barrier.

The Mormons were drawn by duty, occupying an outpost to protect themselves and their religion from the murder and persecution that had driven them out of the Midwest. What had drawn the Anasazis?

In this cut-stone corner of the Colorado Plateau you might guess they were hiding from something. Their ruins are scattered up Butler Wash, Cottonwood Creek, Mule Canyon, and

The San Juan between Bluff Bench and Casa del Eco Mesa, Utah.

Following pages: Bad grazing in the Grand Gulch Primitive Area, Utah.

139

*Remains of a Mormon trading post on the shelf above the San Juan.
It was abandoned when a Navajo killed the owner.*

Chinle Wash. They preferred alcoves facing southwest, where the overhanging cliff shaded them from the summer sun but admitted the low, slanting sunlight of winter. They also seemed to prefer hard-to-see, hard-to-reach sites.

A few years ago I wanted to find such a place as part of the setting for a novel I intended to write. While the plot was nebulous, I planned to have two pot hunters collide in this isolated ruin—one intending to dig up its burials to advance his reputation as a scientist, the other looking for artifacts to sell in order to feed his family. One would kill the other, and my story would pivot on this undetected crime.

Why not simply invent the ruin, just as the pot hunters and the plot are invented? For some reason my imagination doesn't want to stretch that far. It's willing to produce imaginary people doing imaginary deeds only as long as their feet are planted in real landscapes. Or perhaps this is just a rationalization—an excuse I've developed to get away from the word processor and into the places I enjoy. Whatever the real motive, it is my habit to visit the places where I want my fictional events to happen, to stand in the dust, breathe the air, consider the sounds and the smells, watch the light change when the sun goes down, notice the trap-door spider emerge from her hole for her twilight hunt and the bats collecting insects before the moon rises, and listen to the pair of coyotes in coyote conversation on the mesa behind me. Most of it never reaches the page, some of it is modified to fit, but I seem to need such memories when I write a scene.

My quest for this reality led me first to Dan Murphy, one of those U.S. Park Service people who know the empty corners. Murphy knew of an unexcavated ruin that fitted my plot requirements. Getting to it required floating down the San Juan River. That led to Charley and Susan DeLorme, who operate Wild River Expeditions out of Bluff and devote themselves to taking literate folks into interesting places. The DeLormes knew of the cliff house Murphy had described to me and of two or three other suitably isolated ruins where my fictional murder could remain undetected. Getting to these ruins involved a trip down into the San Juan canyon, a walk up one of the washes that drain into it, and then a little climbing. The Anasazis must have used the same route down the river since there's no other way to get there.

As it flows through southern Utah en route to its juncture with the Colorado at Lake

A Wild River Expeditions raft moving down the San Juan toward Mexican Hat.

Slickrock country: Wind and water forming those alcoves the Anasazis loved.

Time has left only traces of this array of Anasazi messages.

An Anasazi cave home downriver from Bluff.

Powell, the San Juan is no stream for daredevil rapid runners. The snow-runoff floods that swept down it in Anasazi times are now controlled by the Navajo Dam in New Mexico. And while the San Juan is the fastest flowing of the major North American rivers (falling eight feet per mile compared with eight inches per mile for the Mississippi), the only risk of dangerous high water comes on those rare days when torrential rain sends a flash flood booming down a side canyon. The San Juan rapids are wild enough only to bounce you around in a raft, drench you with cold spray, or overturn a kayak. The thrill this canyon offers lies in the beauty of its awesome geology.

Eons ago some unimaginable pressure bent the earth's crust upward here, forming a bulge as much as six miles high which geologists call the Monument Upwarp. Over millions of years the top of this vast bubble eroded away, but dramatic traces remain. Comb Ridge is one of them, the remains of the bottom of the eastern edge of the bulge. It extends in a jagged curve almost a hundred miles from the southern border of the Manti-La Sal National Forest west of Blanding, Utah, southeastward to beyond the site of Kayenta, Arizona.

Nine miles downstream from the Red Mesa bridge, the San Juan cuts through Comb Ridge and enters the Lime Ridge anticline. Here the stratified layers of the cliffs slope toward the sky. The river between seems to be pouring sharply downward as if it were draining into the center of the earth. You float here through an engulfing optical illusion, isolated and insulated by the music of water over rock. The sun bakes your back and the river spray chills your face. Geologists love this stretch of river because it sweeps them past the strata that exists at the very bottom of an oil field, giving them a remarkable opportunity to look at the invisible world their drill bits probe.

At the top of the cliffs, worn totally away in many places, is the Morrison formation. Below that, a tan streak of Bluff sandstone, separated from muted Entrada sandstone by the narrow, darker stripe of Wanekah rock. Under that the Carmel deposit lies atop the pale yellow of Navajo sandstone, and below the sandstone is the Kayenta formation. You can count down if you know the litany of the earth's evolution, through the ebb and swell of oceans of the Jurassic age, back into the Triassic, the Permian, and the Pennsylvanian. The layers of the earth, each with its distinctive texture and tone, are exposed like those of a sliced

Lake Powell, where the San Juan drowns in the Colorado, with Navajo Mountain rising on the Arizona border to the south. Following pages: The author's favorite approach to Monument Valley—tough country to farm.

onion: Shinarump marble, Halgaito shale, great red cliffs of Wingate sandstone with stripes of Akah limestone; some smooth, some eroded into weird shapes.

What most intrigues geologists—who sometimes make this float just to see them—are Ismay algae biotherms. Under these domed shapes the black gold of petroleum deposits are found. A couple of miles above Mexican Hat the river cuts directly through such a formation, exposing to the light of day what elsewhere is the deep, rich bottom of the oil fields of the Aneth and Paradox basins. Here the oil has long since drained into the river, and the sandy water laps into the empty stone hemispheres. But only a few miles to the east it is still being pumped from deposits thousands of feet below the surface, a field expected to produce a half billion barrels of oil.

The canyon offers another rare treasure. You can drift down it with a sense of total isolation, thoroughly incommunicado and safe at last from that plague of civilization—the telephone. On many stretches of the river if you beached your kayak carelessly and it was swept away, you would be as hopelessly stranded as a man on the moon. There is no way upstream or down except the river itself and it would drown you. The cliffs that wall you in are impossible to climb. And if you could climb them, your effort would take you to the stony top of a mesa with no place to go and no way to climb back down. Here the empty canyonland edge of Utah abuts an equally empty slice of northern Arizona. You could fire a cannon here and no one would hear it.

Except for the river itself, the only possible routes out of the canyon are the washes that drain into it—and up some of those a few Anasazi families built their little hideaway homes in the dying years of their civilization. The cliff house Murphy had suggested is a mile or so up one of these—invisible from the wash bottom. You find it by climbing from the watercourse to a sandstone ledge from which it is still not visible, and then climbing from

*S*andstone form near the Bisti Badlands, northwest New Mexico.

that to a higher plain of sandstone, earth, and gravel from which high cliffs rise to the top of the mesa. Water pouring down from the mesa top eroded alcoves in the faces of these cliffs, and one of these fit all the usual Anasazi criteria for building sites. It faced so that the low winter sun would warm it while the overhanging cliff shaded it in summer. It was nicely hidden, visible only to those who climbed to the shelf in front of it. And the cliff house, built far back in its shadows, is hard to see even from that vantage point.

It is cool under the alcove. A spring seeps down the cliff in snow-runoff season and during the summer monsoons, watering a

Looking across the San Juan from Utah into the Navajo Reservation.

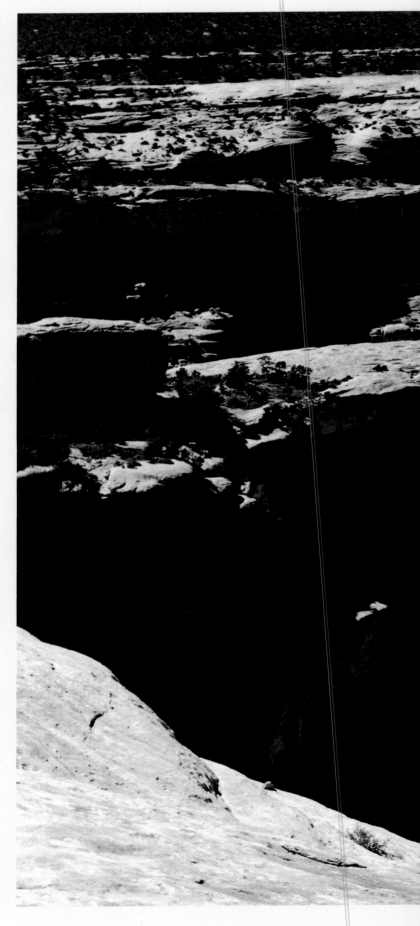

On the rimrock above the saddle, Leaphorn stopped again. He got out his binoculars and spent five minutes examining the landscape. The saddle, as it had appeared from the lake, seemed to be the only easy way down. Beyond the saddle, south of the cliff on which Leaphorn stood, a shelf of land extended from the escarpment. The timber there was a thick jumble of mixed dry-country conifers. He had noticed it before, spotting it as ideal deer cover—the sort of place a deer herd would pick for a resting place. A single neck of land connected this great hill with the mesa. Against the rimrock, the deer could not be approached from above because of the overhung cliff. They could watch the backtrail, as resting deer always did, with no trouble. Rising air currents during the day would carry up to them the scent of any predator. And there were escape routes. The way down was steep but, unlike the mesa cliffs, not impossible.

From Dance Hall of the Dead

◆◆◆

Mountain goats still thrive in this landscape near Montezuma Creek, Utah. Following pages: The San Juan provides a ribbon of rare green in Utah's redrock country.

San Juan rafters pausing to inspect pictographs on a riverside cliff.

heavy growth of fern on the shadowed stone and forming a pool on the alcove floor. For a reason that must have something to do with defense and nothing with convenience, the Anasazi family that lived here built its house on a shelf a dozen feet up the back wall of this amphitheater. High above that, not far below the alcove roof and barely visible from the pool, they built another, smaller structure reachable only by a precarious climb up footholds chipped into the stone. Enemy attackers trying to reach it would have been utterly vulnerable.

In my mind the same question always rises. Enemy attackers?

You sit with your back to the stone exactly as those who built the structures above your head must have sat. You look out of the shadow into the same dazzling hot sunlight. Who was the enemy? Who else lived then on this vacant continent? If the anthropologists and archaeologists know as much as they seem to know, the Anasazis must have had this cut-stone corner of the planet to themselves when this alcove was inhabited. If not the first comers, they were the first to leave their footprints.

So, being a writer of fiction, I sit in the cool shade, watch the rising heat waves make the air shimmer over the sandstone bench, think speculative thoughts, and look for ways to make this place part of the plot I am trying to form. Could those precarious steps cut into the sandstone have a fictional use? That should be easy. How about the hundreds of dark little spadefoot toads hopping around the margin of the pool? Some of them are as big as one's thumbnail, some still have a vestige of the tail they carried from the egg, some are still tadpoles, captives of the water. There are other such desert toads at the little pools left in the wash bottom—attracting the snakes and birds and other predators that feed upon them. But enough will survive to mate and lay their eggs in the drying mud to await next summer's rains, when the eggs will hatch and renew the cycle. How can the life cycle of desert toads relate to that of desert people? How many generations of Anasazis survived in this cool alcove? What predators hunted them? How can either relate to the story I am trying to shape? Ideas come, refuse to fit, and are replaced with other ideas which also refuse to fit. The shadow of the cliff lengthens across the sandstone bench. What use are toads, anyway? Could you

Shade protects an Anasazi ruin near Mexican Hat, Utah, from the fierce July sun.

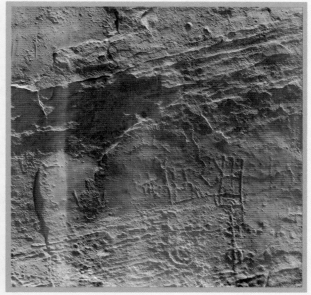

Near its beginnings in the Chuska Mountains, Many Ruins Canyon is cut deep and narrow through the Chinle sandstone formation of that plateau. There its cliffs rise sheer and vertical almost a thousand feet above a narrow, sandy bottom. It is much shallower by the time it emerges into Chinle Valley and becomes a mere drainage wash as it meanders northward toward Utah through the Greasewood Flats. But the cut deepens again in its passage through the Nokaito Bench to the San Juan. Here the crazy mishmash geology of the earth's crust had given Many Ruins a different shape. One climbed out of it on a series of steps. First the low, sometimes earthen cliffs that crowded its narrow streambed, then a broken sandstone shelf hundreds of yards wide, then more cliffs, rising to another shelf, and still more cliffs rising to the flat top of Nokaito Mesa.

From A Thief of Time

◆◆◆

Above: A thousand years of weather leaves only faded remains of Anasazi petroglyphs on a San Juan River cliff. Left: A young alcove just beginning to form in a sandstone cliff near Bluff.

159

*The rim of the Grand Gulch plateau across the San Juan from the Navajo Reservation.
Note the Anasazi dwellings built into the cliff.*

play games with them? A crazy idea, that? Crazy? I find myself imagining a recluse living here, his mind twisted by illness and loneliness, devising a contorted game with toads. Thus the plot of *A Thief of Time* evolves into something I hadn't foreseen.

Finishing that tale required (perhaps I should say warranted) a second trip. There's an Anasazi site called River House a ways down the San Juan from the mouth of Comb Creek. It had been vandalized recently. The small universe of the river allows no secrets, and I was told the vandal was an emotionally disturbed Navajo boy. My imagination transmuted that. A subplot took shape and then there was someone to play games with the spadefoot toads. Upstream from River House, Anasazi artists had pecked an elaborate display of petroglyphs through the dark manganese oxide deposits on the cliff. Much harder work, this, than the pictographs painted in Canyon de Chelly.

I found myself thinking of the artist's hand, holding the sharpened antler, hammering with a rock. Bloody knuckles. The bandaged hand of a woman archaeologist I know came to mind. The Anasazi artist changed gender in my imagination. And in the plot I was trying to shape, the victim became a woman.

Later that evening the splash of the kayak paddle startled a heron from a sandbar's growth of willows. He flies downstream, a graceful white shape in the twilight, and vanishes in the darkness around the river bend. Why is such a bird living in solitude here? Perhaps herons are one of those species that, like wolves and swans, mate for life. Perhaps his mate had died and he grieves for her here. If you happen to be working on a novel, you consider even grief in the context of your story.

That evening after you have your sleeping bag rolled out and you are washing yourself in the river, a beaver comes along, swimming upstream. He looks old and shows no more interest in you than he would in a deer. He stops to rest where a rock deflects the current, exhausted. You can think of no motive for a tired old beaver to be making such a difficult trip into a rocky canyon that seems to offer nothing for him to eat. In the strange way the imagination works, the question of heron and beaver combine to solve a problem in the plot.

Those deeper questions, involving the Anasazis and why they hid themselves in this wilderness of stone, I leave to the anthropologists.

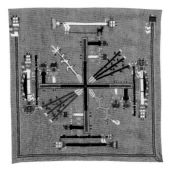

Navajo sand-painting rug.

Goat country near Moenkopi, Arizona.

*A*mid dunes stabilized by Mormon tea, stands a refuge for Navajo youngsters awaiting their school bus ride into Kayenta.
In parts of the reservation, the ride for some children is more than a hundred miles a day.

*F*ollowing pages: An aerial view of scattered Navajo
homesteads linked by dirt roads on the northwest side
of the Big Reservation, where grazing is poor.

The cemetery at Bluff, Utah.

*Near Bluff, on the hottest day anyone can remember.
Following pages: The first soft snow in the Kaibab
Mountains north of the Grand Canyon.*

THE HIGH COUNTRY

◆◆◆

When I was writing *The Fly on the Wall,* I reached a point in the narrative when the protagonist, a political reporter named John Cotton, receives a note giving him a choice—get out of town or die. In the nebulous plan with which I began this book, the hero was to ignore this threat and go about his business of solving the mystery. But by then, having lived with this fellow for five chapters and almost as many months, I knew he was too sensible and cynical for such behavior. He would get out of town. But where would he run?

It was an easy question to answer, and I think it would be for most folks with the same problem. Where would you go if you were tired, discouraged, fearful, and needed a place to relax and restore the spirit? Most of us can close our eyes and remember such a place. I put John Cotton on a plane to New Mexico, rented him a car, and took him to a place I used to go when I needed silence and isolation.

The handful of fishermen who went there called it the Brazos Meadows. It is high country—the watershed of the Brazos River, a short, clear, ice-cold trout stream which comes pouring out of the Brazos Box and quickly disappears into the Chama River. It's a small

Above: The color frost brings in the Santa Fe National Forest.
Left: Tesuque Creek in the Sangre de Cristo Mountains near Santa Fe.

October aspen in the Sangre de Cristo Mountains.

stream, even as streams go in desert states, and should never be confused with the more important Brazos meandering through Texas. Most of its water comes from snowmelt fed into a maze of swampy meadows that sprawl across the Colorado–New Mexico border about a hundred crow-flight miles north of Santa Fe.

The meadows are partly in the Carson National Forest, and thus open to people like myself, and partly in private land which is mostly posted. If you want access you have to know who to ask and how to ask them. The private land was once the Tierra Amarilla land grant. The old Mexican communal grant was sold by an heir long ago, but years passed before other families who thought they still had grazing and wood-cutting rights began finding themselves fenced off. It is now officially the property of the Chama Land and Cattle Company and other ranching outfits, but the rights to it have been the source of a hundred years of acrimony, lawsuits, shootings, barn burnings, fence cuttings, and bitterness handed down from father to son.

It's hard to imagine this great cool, green country as a source of anger. When summer comes, those with grazing permits bring in their flocks of sheep, driving them out again with the first snow. Except for the sheep, a few cows, a rare cowboy, mule deer, hundreds of elk, marmots, black bears, and coyotes, it's one of the emptiest places on the map—and certainly the emptiest one I know of that isn't desert.

My copy of *Guide to New Mexico Mountains* lists the area as the Brazos Mountain Range, but it manages this exaggeration by lumping together three scattered peaks that jut out of a vast rolling expanse of grass-and-forest tableland. The mountains are Broke Off (10,365 feet), Tusas (10,150), and Jawbone (10,680), barely tall enough by Rocky Mountain standards to be listed. They seem even less impressive than they are because they rise from "average terrain" that is unusually lofty. All around are grander mountains—the San Juans to the north, the Sangre de Cristos across the Rio Grande, the Jemez to the southeast. Even San Antonio Mountain, the isolated ash cone of an old volcano poking up from the Rio Grande plateau, looks down on them.

Right: High country above Durango, Colorado.
Following pages: Early snow whitens Dibe'Nitsaa
(Hesperus Peak), which marks the northern boundary
of Navajo Country and is sacred to the tribe.

Silverton: The ore is gone. The beauty remains.

A linotype operator named Woodrow Wilson introduced me to the meadows. Wilson is one of those born to be out-of-doors, a man who knows when sand plums are ripe, where to collect everything from wild asparagus, piñon nuts, and mushrooms to firewood and fossils. I had touched his heart with an account of the bad luck I was suffering on the Pecos and the Chama and other streams in what was then the beginning of my lifelong effort to catch trout. "I'll show you a place you'll get 'em," Wilson said. "Guarantee it."

At that time one reached the section of meadows Wilson favored by making the hundred-mile drive north from Santa Fe to Antonito, Colorado, turning west up the Conejos River valley to the village of Mogote, and there finding a forest service road that headed south—and up. Changing altitudes

The Cumbres & Toltec, the nation's highest railroad, chuffs toward Cumbres Pass.

here means changing biological life zones. The low end of the Conejos valley is not much higher than six thousand feet—the Upper Sonoran life zone of buffalo grass, sagebrush, stream-side cottonwood bosques, and scattered piñon and juniper. As the road climbs, this quickly changes to ponderosa pine and mountain mahogany of the Transition zone, and then to the mixed forests of fir, aspen, and spruce of the Hudsonian. About six miles in from Mogote on this July day, we encountered our first snowbanks, lurking in the deep shade of spruce groves, mostly ice by now and grimy with two months' collection of whatever the wind had deposited. On the protected east slope of Ozier Peak enough of one of these drifts had survived to cover the road, requiring the use of the shovel and tire chains that were part of the permanent equipment in Wilson's battered car.

Even forty years ago shoveling wet snow in the thin air at more than nine thousand feet required me to pause often to gasp for breath. Ozier Peak is a great place for such pauses. It looks down into Toltec Gorge, through which the swift little Los Pinos River races, and up the river valley to Cumbres Pass. Directly (and about a thousand feet) below is Ozier Station. From this lofty perspective it looks like something made for an old-fashioned model train. In those days, the station consisted of a sheep-holding pen with loading ramps, a wooden water tower with its eaves giving shelter to the mud nests of a thousand swallows, and a neat little frame building where a Denver and Rio Grande railroad hand lived during the year until snow stopped the trains and forced him out. Now the sheep pens are abandoned, and the old narrow gauge line, long the nation's highest commercial railroad, has become the

Horses grazing near Tierra Amarillo, New Mexico.

Coming down from South Fork, Colorado, in October.

Trout pool and riffle on the Rio Grande below Creede.

Cumbres and Toltec, with its old steam engines pulling tourists between Chama and Antonito in the no-snow months.

When I first saw it, the road down the steep slope from Ozier Peak to Ozier Station had been pounded out by logging trucks. Loaded, they crawled up a zigzag series of switchbacks. Empty, they cut the corners off these angles as they raced downhill. While going up, one hoped not to meet a logging truck coming down. While down, one hoped that the afternoon rains that fall almost every late-summer day over this range would miss this particular slope. If they hit it, one waited until the road dried. While most of these unimproved high-country roads are difficult when muddy, this one was simply impossible.

Once across the tracks, the road passes between station house and water tower (and immediately past a two-inch pipe from which gushes a stream of the icy spring water), plunges another five hundred yards to the river, crosses a narrow plank bridge over the river, and a smaller plank bridge over a feeder stream, and then climbs the opposite ridge. Over that ridge lie the meadows.

At this altitude, July is still spring. Wild iris bloom in bright blue patches in the marshes, and a billion dandelions speckle the slopes with yellow. The gray-green of spruce and the dark green of fir surround the meadows on every hillside, and through the deep grass a half dozen streams meander. These are what form the Brazos ("arms" in Spanish). I think of them as *dedos* ("fingers" in English). They are too small to be arms. And too small, I thought that first day, for trout. In most places they are virtually invisible, hidden by the lush grass. In many places you can step across them. And when you do, you see skittish little trout, flashing through water as clear as glass, startled by any sign of movement.

The secret, Wilson told me, is in the stalking. He surveyed one of the little streams from afar, looking for pools, for depths where the stream has undercut the bank at a sharp curve. He circled the chosen spot, then crawled toward it through the grass on knees and elbows, cradling a short fly rod on his forearms.

Wilson told me to expect the best strike in each hole on the first cast. He flicked his line, sidearm, toward a hidden pool no more than ten feet away. The breeze caught the hook and it snagged in the grass. He tried again. A splash. A flurry of splashing. Wilson extracted a trout, wriggling silver, perhaps seven inches long. He displayed it. Small, but beautiful.

The Denver & Rio Grande crosses its namesake river en route to Creede.

*Following pages: The high end of San Antonio Creek
in the Jemez Mountains of New Mexico.*

181

I'm told the little trout that proliferate in those little meadow streams are a variation of the eastern brook trout strain. We called them "cutthroats" because of the red stripe under their gills. In those days neither the size nor bag limits applied to them because they reproduced so copiously that they tended to overpopulate the water. What little science was involved in catching them had nothing to do with selecting the lure. If they weren't spooked, they hit anything that moved. Wilson wrapped a bit of tinfoil from his cigarette pack around the shank of his hook. I wrapped mine with red thread raveled from my shirttail. Success required filing the barb from the hook, or pinching it down, so the smaller fish could free themselves from a slack line. It was more hunting than fishing. First you scouted for the deepest holes and undercuts, calculated where the boss trout of the hole would be, and then worked out an approach that dropped the hook in the right spot on the first cast. You usually got a strike with every cast, but the bigger the fish, the wiser, and after that first cast you found yourself dealing with trout not much larger than your thumb.

Wilson and I caught enough keepers to fry for lunch that day, stocked some more in a snowbank to take home, and released scores of others.

But that was forty years ago.

I returned to those meadows summer after summer. Then, thirty years ago, a posted sign appeared beside one of the cattleguards you have to cross. That year I paused to fish the Los Pinos. The next year, a flash flood sent boulders tumbling down the feeder stream and knocked out the little plank bridge with (praise be!) my car parked on the proper side of it.

Road to good fishing north of Chama, New Mexico.

When I came back two summers later, the bridge over the Los Pinos itself had been swept away. The sawmill was gone now and so were the logging trucks. The bridge was never replaced. I found another way into the meadows on a road that wanders around San Antonio Mountain, follows San Antonio Creek upstream, passes a cowboy's line shack, and then drops down to the Brazos. The stream is bigger here, and so were the cutthroats, but the cowboy rode up and told me the place was posted but that someone had stolen the signs. The next year I followed two grass-grown tracks down another hillside and found a long-abandoned mine and a smaller meadow where a dozen springs feed a stream called Diablo Creek that drains down a cliff into the Los Pinos. It was the Fourth of July, but I fished all day without hearing a human voice.

The author at work on San Antonio Creek in the Jemez Mountains.

What the mining boom left behind, near Creede, Colorado.

*Mine waste and autumn aspen in
the San Juan Mountains.*

HILLERMAN COUNTRY

North, over Sleeping Ute Mountain in Colorado, over Utah's Abajo Mountains, great thunderheads were reaching toward their evening climax. Their tops, reflecting in the direct sun, were snowy white and the long streamers of ice crystals blown from them seemed to glitter. But at lower levels the light that struck them had been filtered through the clouds over the Chuskas and turned into shades of rose, pink, and red. Lower still, the failing light mottled them from pale blue-gray to the deepest blue. Overhead, the streaks of high-level cirrus clouds were being ignited by the sunset. They drove through a fiery twilight.

From Coyote Waits

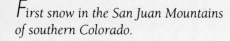

*A*nasazi black-on-white jar.

*F*irst snow in the San Juan Mountains
of southern Colorado.

189

Trujillo Meadows near Cumbres Pass, in the Colorado–New Mexico borderlands.

Autumn in a quiet corner northeast of Chama, New Mexico.

Now Ozier Station has become a lunch stand for tourists riding the Cumbres and Toltec sightseeing train. When I returned years later to Diablo Creek, a watermelon was cooling in my favorite hole, and three families were having a picnic. The Chama Land and Cattle Company has added to its beef business the operation of a luxury fishing and hunting resort where the affluent are provided personal guides to the good places and can shoot an elk for a few thousand dollars.

The beauty is still there, of course. I suspect that the grouse still raise their chicks on the slope below Ozier Station, and the marmot colony still whistles defiance at passersby along the West Fork of the Brazos, and the summer clouds still leave some of their mist behind in the tops of the firs when they drag their bottoms over the rim of Broke Off Mountain. But I don't go there any longer. I would rather remember it the way it used to be.

*Above: A cowboy's abandoned shack in the
San Juan Mountains.
Left: Almost winter at the edge of the San Juan National Forest.
Following pages: Late-summer grazing, southwest Colorado.*

The cottonwoods along the river formed a crooked line of dazzling gold across a vast landscape of grays and tans. And beyond, the dark blue mountains formed the horizon, the Abajos, Sleeping Ute, and the San Juans, already capped with early snow. It was one of those still, golden days of high desert autumn.

From Coyote Waits

◆◆◆

Above: Tree with half moon.
Left: Summer's end on the River of
Lost Souls (Animas) in southern Colorado.

197

Church near Antonito, Colorado.

Early frost on the Conejos River, southern Colorado.

The upper Chama in fly-fishing season.

Aspen turning near Slumgullion Pass in Colorado.

REMEMBERED PLACES

◆◆◆

I t seems strange but it's true, as Conrad Richter once told us, that something as inanimate as a place can inspire love. Richter made that statement in an essay written about thirty years ago, commenting on the effect of the Plain of San Agustin in central New Mexico.

"The beauty, the mystery, the immensity of that grassland got into my blood," Richter wrote. It inspired *The Sea of Grass*, which brought to him the Pulitzer prize and to us one of the greatest novels in which landscape is as important as character.

Other writers have put it in other ways. D. H. Lawrence said the view from his ranch in the Sangre de Cristo Mountains above Taos "changed me forever," liberating him from modern civilization. "The moment I saw the brilliant, proud morning shine high up over the deserts of Santa Fe, something stood still in my soul, and I attended." Haniel Long described this odd love affair more specifically—remembering a tiny village in the Santa Fe River canyon. "I see it all again; and yet, can these houses be so red? And the dogs the children play with, can they be so white? And the Cerrillos hills seen through an arroyo leading skyward, can they be so blue? And when one goes to it between the walls of blue rock, one may really not be going to it at all, but rather dreaming a dream he has dreamt before. Surely no one

Above: House and sunset on the Colorado plateau.
Left: A dawn flight of cranes over the Bosque Del Apache marshes.

Blue grama blades trace the work of shifting winds.

can be sure he has visited Cienega; people say to themselves, do they not: 'Was it a vision; or have I, some time or other, seen dusk in a valley like this?'"

In his *Man Made of Words,* N. Scott Momaday, another Pulitzer-winning novelist whose works are rich with love of landscape, tells us that everyone should collect the treasures of such a place in memory. "He ought to look at it from as many angles as he can, to wonder about it, to dwell upon it. He ought to imagine that he touches it with his hands at every season and listens to the sounds that are made upon it. He ought to imagine the creatures that are there and all the faintest motions of the wind. He ought to recollect the glare of noon and all the colors of dawn and dusk."

Most of us, I think, follow Momaday's advice. I have my own storeroom of such places—places I can visit without leaving my chair. In my case, they tend to be seasonal.

White Sands National Monument, for example, has a special appeal for me in the winter. I remember it as I first saw it—a February night in 1953. I had driven down the Tularosa Basin, with the snowcapped Sacramentos looming to the east, and to the west mile after mile of tumbled lava—the outpouring of volcanic vents north of the village of Carrizozo. The map shows three communities in the fifty-five miles between Carrizozo and Alamogordo, the first being Oscuro. I'd stop there and take a break. But Oscuro proved to be an unoccupied house beside the railroad track. I would stop, instead, at Three Rivers. But Three Rivers was also a single building, a service station closed for the day. A sign there pointed up a dirt road toward a recreational area. I followed it. It led eastward to what has now been declared the Three Rivers Petroglyph National Recreational Site. Even before official federal recognition it was an impressive place—an upthrust of magma-formed grassy ridges, topped with great black boulders. The highest ridge provides a superb lookout spot for anyone wanting a broad view of the basin. Stone Age hunters had used it as a campsite for their hunts. While waiting for game they chipped into the basalt hundreds of shapes—representations of reptiles, animals, spirits, and men in styles that suggest Klee and Picasso, geometric forms, symbols, even what seem to be pure abstractions. As I remember it was on this ridge that I first noticed White Sands.

Far to the southeast between me and the Organ Mountains was a long, white line shimmering in the late afternoon sun.

*R*idge line of the Organ Mountains above dunes at White Sands.

*F*ollowing pages: Fishermen's church
below Navajo Dam, New Mexico.

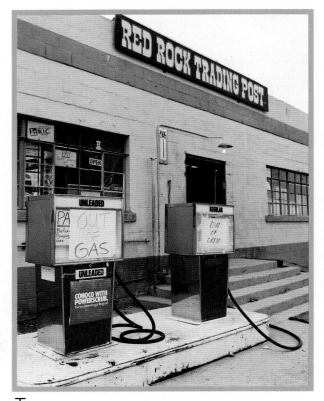

*T*rading post at Red Rock, Arizona, showing why one keeps gas tanks full while driving reservation roads.

Highway 70 intersects this whiteness on its way to the mountain pass between Alamogordo and Las Cruces. The National Park Service visitors center beside the highway was unmanned on this winter evening. Past it, the access road leads through a gray-white saltbush flat. Then the dunes rise around you. Plants endure at the edges, iodine bush, creosote, saltbush, skunkbush sumac, soaptree yucca, rubber pennyroyal—perennials and grasses of heroic tolerance for drought and toxic chemicals. But within a few hundred yards the plants are gone. You are surrounded by a landscape of undulating white. All around you are great dunes, some as high as three-story buildings, their southwest slopes gradual and carved by the wind, their northwest faces smooth and soft. There is nothing quite like it elsewhere on planet Earth.

White Sands is not sand at all, not that tawny mixture of pulverized stone and silicate which forms the usual desert dune. It is gypsum, almost pure, which has been leaching for the past million years out of the Organ Mountains and draining into what geologists call Lake Lucero. The "lake" proper is a ten-mile-long playa that collects runoff and seepage from the mountains. The desert sun burns away the moisture, leaving a layer of deposited gypsum crystals. The prevailing southwesterly wind cuts into the back of these dunes, pushing dislodged crystals up to the crest, where they tumble down. Thus the dune moves with inexorable slowness, burying all before it. For something like a million years this combination of rain, sun, and wind has moved a sheet of gypsum crystals toward the north and west, forming a white desert that now covers more than 270 square miles.

The moon was about three-quarters full that night, rising early over the Sacramentos, its light reflecting off the snow pack on distant Sierra Blanca and from the glittering gypsum. Away from the access road, you can climb the hard side of a dune to its crest and see no sign that the planet is inhabited. Alamogordo and the headquarters buildings of the missile research center that shoots its rockets down the desert range are too far away to be visible. The silence is absolute, the world around you as dead as the gypsum below your feet, the nearest human a long day's walk away. You might be on another planet, the only survivor of a crashed spacecraft. Stranded. Alone.

*I*n Socorro, New Mexico.
Following pages: The San Marcial
Marshes south of Socorro.

Another of my favorite winter places is as alive as White Sands is dead. It's called Bosque del Apache and the time to be there is a January dawn, after an arctic cold front has driven migratory waterfowl out of their feeding places in the Dakotas, Wyoming, and Colorado.

When I first saw the place, U.S. Highway 85 ran right beside it, following the Rio Grande southward en route to Mexico City. The "Woods of the Apaches" had always been on the travel route of many besides the birds who make it their way station. Before the Spanish came through it in the sixteenth century, Indian trails had crossed here. The Mescalero Apaches used it regularly as a camping place and gave

Canada and snow geese starting their long flight north up the Rio Grande valley.

it its name. It was the route of the Camino Real, the link between Chihuahua and the Spanish outpost at Santa Fe. But no one, Indian, Spanish, Mexican, or American, ever managed to settle here permanently. The river is hospitable upstream and down, flowing between miles of irrigated fields. But here between the San Cristobal Range and the San Mateo Mountains, it withdraws its invitation. The Piro Indians moved in and left a ruined pueblo to mark their failure. The Spanish tried, but only dots on old maps show where their communities died out. San Marcial, the little town that gives the adjoining marshes their name, was built twice and twice erased by devastating spring floods of the Rio Grande. Nothing of those efforts remains except the name. The Mexican government gave all of it—the final land grant before the American occupation—to Antonio Sandoval in the hope he could establish a permanent settlement. He couldn't. Anglo-American settlers established the town of Clyde beside the marshes. A flood swept away all but the foundations. John Chisholm seized it as part of his cattle empire. Finally, during the Great Depression, it fell into the hands of the federal government and became a game refuge. It is now, as it must have been when the Piros built their ill-fated pueblo, the winter home of hundreds of thousands of migratory birds and of most varieties of the mammals of the Rocky Mountain West.

The highway has moved away from the river now, the divided four lanes of Interstate 25 cutting a broad swath through the creosote bush on the slope of the Coyote Hills. But the narrow pavement that was U.S. 85 is still there, used only by bird watchers and the few farmers who get free use of the Bosque land in return for leaving half their crops to feed the wildlife. Grass sprouts through the old road's cracks here and there and nibbles at its margins, nature's reminder that the works of man are transient.

The Rio Grande near Los Lunas with clouds covering Sandia Crest at Albuquerque.

Ranch barn near Durango, Colorado.

Foothills of the San Juan Mountains.

215

Franciscan mission church in Zuni.

In those black moments just before dawn the silence here is almost total. Traffic on I-25 is light as well as distant, and long moments pass with no sound at all. Then you begin hearing an odd murmur. The river, you think, or perhaps the San Marcial Ditch, which parallels it to carry water to irrigated fields far downstream. But they are a half mile away. And this isn't the sound of moving water. It is the conversation of birds.

Thousands upon thousands of them awaken in the marshes and under the winter-bare cottonwoods. You distinguish the odd fluting call of sandhill cranes, the shrill note of red-winged blackbirds, the deeper note of geese, and a mixture of sounds of scores of other species. It is a small sound at first, scattered and episodic. But it grows. And about when the sun creates a red glow behind the Oscura Mountains to the east, you hear the sound of wings.

The snow geese are first, rising off the ponds to breakfast in the sorghum fields up the river. Twenty thousand of them, perhaps more, great white birds with black wing tips rising out of the darkness into the rosy reflected light of dawn. They make a sweeping turn, a cloud of wings rising above the cottonwoods. But cloud is the wrong word. They don't form a disorderly blackbird rabble but a kaleidoscope of goose formations, always shifting, but always orderly. The light catches them—white against the tan velvet of the hills. Then they are overhead, line after line, layer above layer of formations, and the sky is filled with the clamor of an infinity of geese.

The Canada geese are overhead now as well, and the great gray shapes of the sandhill cranes in their long, even lines (eleven thousand was the crane count that year) and finally the laggard ducks in a dozen varieties, sometimes in twos, but usually hurrying somewhere in their version of the V formation. I think this is how it must have been when the Mescalero Apaches made their campfires here.

There are autumn places, too.

In the dry and windy spring of 1887, sheep herders let a campfire get out of hand in Big Tesuque Canyon, in the mountains above Tesuque, New Mexico. It burned the slopes of Santa Fe Baldy, Lake Peak, and Aspen Peak. It became so spectacular that authorities in the territorial capital at Santa Fe sent a telegram to the secretary of the interior asking for funds to put the fire out. A wire came back asking for a cost estimate. The estimate was $600. No funds came, and the fire burned through May, June, and July, stopping at the timberline for lack of fuel but crossing the high passes into Holy Ghost Canyon, then across Pecos Baldy

Sandhill cranes near Socorro with South Baldy wearing its winter cap.

*Following pages: Bosque del Apache Marsh
with the Coyote Hills in the background.*

I n the high, dry mountains of the Colorado Plateau, fog is out of its element. It forms as part of a climatic accident, produced when a cold front crosses a mountain range and collides with warmer air on the opposite slope. And it survives no longer than a fish out of water. By dawn, when the four of them reached the place of Hosteen Begay, the fog had already lost its character as a solid blinding cloud. Now it survived only in pockets, as patches and fragments.

From The Ghostway

♦♦♦

Since the sight of actual Kachina spirits by a human is dangerous, they remain invisisble. They are represented by masked dancers and carved figures such as this.

Misty morning south of Pagosa Springs, Colorado.

Trees at Aspen Basin above Santa Fe.

and into the Las Vegas Range. There, helped by the rains of August, a timberman providing ties for the railroad took in a crew and put out the fire.

You can still find fire-killed logs left by that blaze in the Pecos Wilderness Area. When fir and spruce are burned away, meadows form in the ashes—first grasses, then perennial bushes, and finally aspen. The aspen stand until they are crowded out by the conifers moving in again to recapture the mountain. The healing of that great 1887 burn is approaching that final stage now. The world's premier aspen forest still stands on the slopes of Lake, Aspen, and Tesuque peaks. When autumn arrives here, the gold of aspen dazzles the mind.

Starting in late September, the great splash of yellow is visible from Interstate Highway 25 as far away as the top of La Bajada, more than twenty miles south of Santa Fe and at least thirty miles from those three mountains. The road leading to the Santa Fe ski basin cuts just below the old burn. You can park where it crosses Tesuque Creek. Walk up the slope two hundred yards and you can be, as D. H. Lawrence put it, "liberated from modern civilization."

You are immersed in a world of white, black, and yellow, and the dazzling yellow overpowers you. The ground beneath you is a mat of fallen aspen leaves—a uniform bright gold. Above you, the sunlit roof of unfallen leaves is an even brighter yellow. Look right or left, behind you or straight ahead, and you look into a maze of straight white aspen trunks, their chalky bark punctuated with black scarring. On the still day, the only motion is an occasional leaf fluttering downward. But even on the stillest day, enough air moves to make its music in the trees. If you take time to listen, you can always hear an aspen forest talking.

There are other places (and times) engraved in the memory. One is a windless twilight where the Rio Grande has sliced its spectacular gorge through the sagebrush flats west of Taos. The river is invisible here, the top of its narrow canyon hidden behind a fold of the prairie, but you hear its voice. Seven hundred feet below you, where the spring runoff is raging and booming over polished basalt boulders, the sound would be deafening. Standing here in the sagebrush, your ears detect only a murmur seeming to come from beneath your feet, as if the earth were muttering in its sleep.

*Autumn color in the
Santa Fe National Forest.*

Above: Cottonwoods in the Rio Grande Bosque.
Right: The forest floor in autumn.

Zia vase.

L eaphorn leaned back against the rock, squirmed into an easier position. Above him the sky was turning gray. The overcast had been building since noon. First it was nothing more than high-altitude humidity —a thin layer of stratospheric ice crystals which hung a glittering halo around the sun. Then a semiopaque grayness had crept in from north-northwest and the day gradually lost its light.

From Dance Hall of the Dead

◆◆◆

A thunderstorm over Santa Fe Baldy, east of Tesuque.

227

*A*uthor and friend at Big Mountain, Arizona.

Then there is the volcanic ray that wanders like the Great Wall of China southward from Ship Rock. Navajo Route 33 cuts through this thin stone barrier en route to Red Rock, making access to it easy for those of us who enjoy such geological oddities and lonely places. The molten magma squeezed up through the cracked earth is thirty or forty feet high but only about three feet thick. A million years of frost and heat have cracked it, and chunks have fallen out. On the day I most like to remember, the gusting wind was fluting through these little windows. The wind was the advance guard of a thunderstorm sweeping eastward out of Arizona. It bombarded Beautiful Mountain with lightning and sent dust devils skittering across the prairie. Down the wall to the north, the core of old Ship Rock volcano rose a thousand feet against the sky, like a free-form version of a Gothic cathedral. Gothic, too, was the color—the stone almost as black as the ominous sky and, balanced on the wind just over the wall, a red-tailed hawk hunting a rodent to kill.

I would want it to look exactly like this if I were illustrating the deeds done by Monster Slayer here in the time of Navajo myth. Monster Slayer, climbing the vertical stone of Ship Rock toward the nest of the Winged Monsters to kill them and make this landscape safe for the Navajos. Monster Slayer, at the nest, teaching the Monsters' chicks to become the eagle and the owl. Monster Slayer rescued from his impossible perch by the sacred Spider Woman.

*C*ochiti storytellers and drummer boy.

*S*hip Rock with windmill, leaky
tank and graffiti.

The world's largest radio telescope, dwarfed by the immense emptiness of the plains of San Agustin near Magdelena, New Mexico.

The list of such places could go on and on: The red stone village of Zuni on Shalako night—reverently playing host to the towering Messenger Birds and the Council of the Gods and feeding thousands of curious visitors on mutton stew and canned peaches. The low sandstone cliff along Dinebito Wash, decorated with a thousand yards of Anasazi pictographs that tell me things I can't quite understand. The long pool in the San Juan below Navajo Dam, at day's end when your legs are cold in your waders. Just as you realize it is too dark to see your lure the trout begin rising all around you, dorsal fins sliding across the current, making sudden splashes as they feed on whatever insect is hatching.

Too dark, but there is always tomorrow. Fishing offers infinite opportunities for hope. Just as our country—Barney's and mine and yours—still offers silent, empty places that revive the spirit.

*L*ow water, low hopes on the Chama River
near Los Ojos, New Mexico.

*T*he middle Chama, above Abiquiu, New Mexico.
Following pages: Rio Grande valley farmland
on a cold winter morning.

ACKNOWLEDGMENTS

My thanks to my wife and traveling companion, Irene, for never complaining of heat, cold, or long hours and for keeping me from becoming utterly and completely lost on numerous occasions. And to the friendly and gracious people throughout the area, too numerous to mention, especially since most of my notes have been misplaced. And thanks to my associate, John Thorne, for keeping my business going while I was traveling and for his great work on the production of the guide prints for the book. Thanks to Dean Doerr for his enthusiastic encouragement, and also to well-known author and photographer Fred Huston for deterring me from including a photograph of a Model A Ford which he thoroughly detested.

Barney Hillerman

The publishers would like to thank the following people and organizations for their help in the preparation of this book:

John Michel, Laurie Wertz, Stephanie Sherman, Richard VanOosterhout, Sigrid Chase, Amy Morton, Katherine Stimson, Bob Firken, Helen Cooney, Rapid Lasergraphics.

Courtesy of Arizona State Museum, University of Arizona, Helga Teiwes, photographer:
Page 38, Anasazi painted quiver, Catalog #L-101c; Page 55, Anasazi black-on-white bowl, Catalog #L-102c; Page 70, Anasazi pots, Catalog #C-5213c; Page 81, Anasazi woven pot rest, Catalog #L-103c; Page 88, Anasazi handled bowl, Catalog #C-7337c; Page 91, Anasazi pitchers, Catalog #C-6299c; Page 189, Anasazi black-on-white jar, Catalog #L-104c.

Photographs from Manley-Prim Photography:
Page 20, Hopi basket; Page 110, Hopi coiled basket; Page 132, Navajo Ganado Red rug; Page 161, Navajo sand-painting rug; Page 227, Zia vase; Page 228, Cochiti storytellers and drummer boy.

Sunset and Ponderosa pines near Pagosa Springs.

INDEX